# FAMILY
# AND
# TELEVISION

# FAMILY AND TELEVISION

*By*

Amarjeet Mahajan
Nirupama Luthara

GYAN

Family and Television

Amarjeet Mahajan
Nirupama Luthara
ISBN : 978-81-212-0435-4

First Published 1993, reprint 2018 in India by
Gyan Publishing House
5, Ansari Road
Daryaganj, New Delhi-110002
Phone: 9811692060
E-mail: books@gyanbooks.com

*Printed at:* G. Print Process, Delhi.

# CONTENTS


CHAPTER 1

Introduction 1

CHAPTER 2

Families Watch Television 33

CHAPTER 3

Television and Children 65

CHAPTER 4

Programmes and Their Evaluation 84

CHAPTER 5

A Resume 115

*Appendix* 134

*References* 136

*Index* 145

# 1

# Introduction

The accessibility of communication satellites and transmission of foreign television programmes have not only revolutionalized the communication system but have also posed a serious threat to our social and cultural ethos. The availability of cable television programmes has also threatened the monopoly of Doordarshan. Additionally cable network is likely to drain off its revenue. It is believed that there are 22,40,000 cable viewers in Delhi alone and cable networks have deprived Doordarshan of Rs. 20 crores revenue from commercials (The Tribune, April 24, 1992). Because of numerous regional languages Doordarshan has no immediate threat. Nevertheless, its chances of a bright survival depends upon the quality of its programmes being transmitted from Delhi Doordarshan as well as decentralization of programme production. As per P.C. Joshi Committee recommendations, the programme contents should be oriented to preserving, consolidating and enriching our unique way of life, customs and traditions. It is through its programmes that Doordarshan can carve out for itself a permanent niche in the lives of its viewers. We should not, however, forget that as we enter the 21st century, communication and information technology will soon change the shape of television programming and viewership. It is high time that we explicate the effectiveness of Doordarshan programmes on the viewers.

By communication we mean flow of material, information perceptions and understanding between various parts and members of society. It includes listening, writing, speaking, reading, channel networks etc. (Vardaman & Halterman, 1968). Communication is also defined as a process of transmitting information, thoughts, opinions, messages, facts ideas or emotions and understanding from one person, place or thing to another person, place or thing (Mamoria, 1987). The word 'communication' has been derived from the Latin word "communis" which stands for common. It thus refers to the sharing of ideas, facts, opinion and understanding with people (Kazmier, 1977).

The members of a society have certain needs to fulfil for which they depend on others. For this purpose they interact with each other. This interaction leads to formation of relationships. A relationship involves a series of interaction in time. For example— A responds to B with behaviour X, whereas B responds to A with the behaviour Y. These individuals interact with each other, binded by the normative patterns of society, which make the relationship stable. The relationship also requires expectations, goals, directions, values, feelings, cognitions etc. However, the type of relationship varies according to the nature of participants and these may vary with individual's specific experiences (Hinde, 1979).

When it comes to the interactions at mass level, this is taken care by mass media of communication. Mass communication is technologically and institutionally based on mass production, mass distribution and mass consumption of public messages in the modern setting. The media of communication are books, magazines, newspapers, journals, radio, films and television. The media disseminates information to reach thousands and millions of people (Fedler, 1978).

For the purpose of proper understanding of mass media of communication, it can be divided in three parts: (1) Written (Newspapers, magazines, journals, books, brochures etc.) ; (2) Audio (Radio) and (3) Audio-visual (Television and Cinema).

The written communication is always in the form of books, newspapers, circulars, journals or in the form of pictorial messages, handouts, notices etc. Vast geographical area, illiteracy, poverty, multiplicity of languages and absence of adequate communication facilities are the causes of its remaining at the back seat of national development in India.

The audio medium has played a significant role in the dissemination of knowledge to the masses, though it has not been able to achieve full success in achieving the national objectives. However, it is directed towards national development programmes such as in the fields of education, agriculture, health, family planning, national integration, social and cultural development.

Technological development in the shape of audio-visual

techniques ushered in 'Information Revolution' which had mass appeal. The cinema and television have played an important role in making the people aware about different social problems, though their main aim was to entertain people. Cinema and television continue to be the most powerful media of mass communication.

Communication Satellites have precipitated the information revolution. 'Information revolution' was ushered in India after the launching of satellite system. With the development of network system television relay covers between 80-85 per cent of Indian population. The accessibility of the information at mass level has revolutionalized the system of communication dissemination and monitoring of knowledge to masses at a given period of time. Television as a medium, through which the new knowledge is made available to general masses, is likely to act as a reinforcer of the traditional value system or an agent of change. Based on such an assumption programmes for different target groups have been envisaged and are being screened on Doordarshan. The present study is limited to finding out the role of television contents in bringing about changes in the life style of the viewers. Despite the threat from cable networks to Doordarshan monopoly the State (in India) has complete control over television transmission. It would be worthwhile to examine its contents, aims, functioning and influence. Hence, we shall confine ourselves to television viewing and its impact on the viewers.

**Development of television in India**

In India television was introduced 25 years after its invention and 30 years after its inception. It still appears to be in a formative stage as a medium of comunication. The television era in India began modestly on September 15, 1959 as a medium of education, rural and community development. The programmes were telecast twice a week for a duration of one hour. The educational programmes for Delhi schools were taken up in 1961. Agricultural informative programmes were started in 1967 entitled 'Krishi Darshan'.

Gradually television centres were commissioned at Bombay, Srinagar, Amritsar, Calcutta, Madras, Lucknow, Pune and duration of transmission was also increased. The overwhelming response from the people resulted in gradually extending the hours of transmission from every centre. The programme content began to include features on formal and non-formal education, new agricultural practices, health, hygiene and nutrition, programmes for children, youth and women including the programmes on drama, music, dance etc. News bulletins and current affairs programmes were included from seven major centres in local language, besides Hindi and English at National level. Films and film based programmes were also included on public demand.

SITE (Satellite Instructional Television Experiment) was first visualized and suggested by Dr. Vikram Sarabhai, the founder of Indian space programme in the mid sixties. SITE as a pilot project was first conceived in 1967-69. It came in operation for a year during 1975-76 (Acharya, 1987).

In April 1976, Doordarshan was given a separate entity from All India Radio. The day also marked the beginning of commercials on television, the revenues from which are ploughed back for Doordarshan's software development. On 15th August, 1982, National network became a reality, Insat IA became operational, coloured television was introduced and use of Microwave links for television were a few major achievements. On 30th August 1983, Insat IB was launched. In February 1987, morning transmission was started named as Breakfast TV, and on 26th January 1989 afternoon transmission was introduced for the housewives.

The future retrospects are to have full fledged studios in all the States of India. Presently there are 19, and there is a target for 49. Further, there will be three tier service i.e.

National, Regional and local. There would be a special North-East television service and country wide exclusive channel for education. There has been a tremendous increase in the television viewers in India. This can be seen with reference to the number of families possessing television sets. In the year 1983, there were 2.73 million television sets, and its number increased to 20 million in the year 1989. The area and population covered by television transmission in 1983 was 7 per cent and 19 per cent respectively. In 1987 it was 48 per cent and 72 per cent. In 1989 it increased to 53 per cent and 75 per cent respectively. At present it covers 70 per cent area and 82 per cent population.

In which way this tremendous growth of television has affected viewer's life style, time budgeting, social habits etc. would be the main thrust of the study.

It is generally believed that television has become a very powerful medium and its contents can mould, reshape people's tastes, likings, social habits etc. However, there is another school of thought which contends that its programmes would become meaningful only when they conform to the value system of our society. In short, television plays two main functions :

1. It can acquaint people with the latest development and through the audio-visual mechanism, it has greater appeal. The programmes on health, education, family planning and welfare etc. are likely to create a new awareness among the people regarding their sole responsibilities. Similarly, the commercials have created a felt need among people to go for the latest products.
2. It can also act as an agent of revivalisation, e.g. the popularity of two epic stories of Ramayana and Mahabharatha shown on Indian television stands as a testimony.

Television in India is completely under the control of Ministry of Information and Broadcasting. The time, programme contents, the commercials, news item, serials, movies, debates, everything which is screened, is regulated, controlled and censored by government machinery before they are screened to the viewers. The Government is also considering to take appropriate legal measures to regulate cable networks (The Tribune, April 25, 1992). So far as Doordarshan is concerned the Government of India has clearly specified three functions and all its programmes are oriented to attain these objectives.Keeping in view the target groups, the programmes are tailored to attain the professed objectives. For example, University Grants Commission (U.G.C.) programme is directed towards the Higher Secondary School children to educate them on different issues pertaining to their course outlines. Similarly, 'Krishi Darshan' as an informative programme is meant for the agriculturalists and other rural people. Let us now look at the functions of television in India as identified by Government of India.

**Functions of Television in India**

The main functions of television in India are:

Information; education; and entertainment.

(1) Information has an important role to play in the process of development of society. It is through television and other media that members of society are given the relevant information regarding the current affairs. Television news is an important source of information. It is also an agency of on going socialization. This means that television content serves as a social teacher. Its curriculum, its thematic content and textual structure have the capacity to create meaning, coherent symbolic world of events, people and objects (Dahlgren, 1977). There are various other programmes which provide information in the fields of science and technology, agriculture, horticulture, health, family planning, food and nutri-

tion, ecology, environment, events of world and other current social issues.

(2) Television content is fast becoming the chief agent of educating the masses. This does not mean merely the transfer of body of knowledge or skills, but this lays emphasis on the development of the individuals by making them aware of what lies beyond their own environment, outside their own knowledge, their own specialization while making them conscious of possibilities and happenings (Groombridge, 1972). There are educational programmes from U.G.C. which are telecast twice a day to help the school going children to learn basic concepts and skills. For adults also, there are some educational programmes for general masses relating to health, food and nutrition, family planning, hygiene, agriculture etc. which can be termed as educative as well as informative.

(3) As a source of entertainment, television content amuses and relaxes. It breaks the monotony of daily life. It is useful against loneliness and isolation. It also presents a fantasy world in which all dreams come true. Feature films, documentaries, serials, plays, dance, music etc. are oriented for the entertainment of the masses.

In addition to the above noted professed functions television transmission is also responsible for promoting consumerism. Since television in India was made commercial, it has become a boon for commercial houses which use the medium to push up their sale and hence profit. In order to increase the sale of their products they invest a large sum on advertisements and sponsored programmes. These commercial advertisements precede all the entertaining programmes. Television in a way promotes consumerism. Advertising creates demands for cosmetics, different dresses, exotic foods, kitchen gadgets and luxury goods etc. Doordarshan earned only Rupees 31 crore in 1984-85 from advertisements. Its revenue has surpassed Rupees 254 crore from commercials during 1990. Both feature films and programmes based on these contributed Rs. 126 crore followed by Hindi serials yielding approximately Rs.100 crore (The Tribune, Feb. 17, 1991). Its revenue has gone up to Rs. 350 crore.

To what an extent these broad functions of television have been attained? This is another area which the present study will explore.

**Television and its Contents**

At the outset we wish to clarify that we are not treating television as a machine technology facilitating social change but its software, contents and programmes prepared by individuals. Bell (1976) has emphasized the importance of "intellectual technology" in his 'post industrial' theory. Post-industrialism, according to Bell is an economy based upon "intellectual technology" and growth in the delivery of services. Whereas the pre-industrial economy is a "game nature", the industrial economy is a "game against the fabrication of the nature", the post-industrial economy is a game between persons where "intellectual technology" replaces "machine technology". William (1982) has drawn somewhat similar conclusions about what he calls "information" based economy or "information technologies". The fundamental premise of the "information revolution" is that the contemporary explosion in communication technologies is changing the nature of human environment. It may, however, be added that it is not the television technology which would act as a catalyst or intensifier of social change. It must be kept in mind that television contents are created by individuals whose job is to maintain the interest of the viewers. In order to do this they must attract and maintain a large and heterogenous audience (Wilson, 1981).

It is not because of access of television programmes to a

large number of viewers at a given time but because of their immediacy and visual drama that television has greater appeal (Comstock, 1980). We can hear what people say to each other and we can hear and see how they use their voices, faces, hands and bodies. The creators of television programmes use nearly all the communication codes of face to face interaction and add to them filmic codes not available in everyday life. It is through well planned software that everyday life is artfully construed and conveyed on television (Dorr, 1986). Fiske (1989), on the other hand, perceives television as a cultural commodity. A programme, according to him, is a commodity produced and then sold to the distributors. In distribution its role changes and it becomes not a commodity, but a producer and what it produces is a new commodity, the audience which is then, in its turn, sold as a commodity to advertisers. It is in the light of these explanations that we will review the literature available indicating different views regarding the impact of television viewing.

**Effects of Television Viewing**

Albrecht (1954) postulated that media might be considered as agents of social change. According to this view the media are thought to be active in bringing about changes in the attitudes or behaviours of the mass audience. Schramm (1964) advocated for making mass media a two-way process. He contended: "Information must flow not only to the television viewers but also from them, so that their needs can be known and they may participate in the decision making process". Television, according to Hirsch (1971), serves as a major communication link between groups, collecting together the members of different tastes, cultures for common exposure to the larger, dominant popular culture. It acts as an integrative influence in the society. McCormack (1981) opines that mass media information plays a peculiar teacher's role, that of a 'history-teacher', who by presenting a coherent version of contemporary history--even refines the historic sensibility of his audience. Noelle-Neumann (1981) after reviewing empirical studies in the Federal Republic of Germany (now Germany) maintained that mass communication information is no mirror but a moulder of opinions and attitudes in the population.

To bring about desired social change people must be informed, persuaded and educated. The 'free and adequate' flow of information could serve to widen horizons, enlist support for social change, raise aspirations, enforce social norms and modify attitudes (Hartmann et. al., 1989). In addition to its use in formal education and in agriculture, literacy and health campaigns, the medium of television has also been used to create an awareness about different social issues of the society. Results of different empirical studies conducted in India highlight positive effects of television viewing. Health programmes of television in India not only created health awareness among the viewers but helped them to launch a cleanliness drive (Agrawal, 1978; Agrawal and Malek, 1986; Jesudasan cited by Gupta, 1986; Sinha, 1985).

Scholars have not only identified the positive effects of television viewing but also its negative effects. Johnson (1967) reported that 60 per cent of the families changed their sleeping patterns because of television. Further 55 per cent altered their meal time. Robinson (cited by Liebert and Sprafkin, 1988) using the technique of time budget found out the effects of television viewing. The activities that decreased were sleep, social gathering away from home, other leisure activities, conversation and household care. Neena Behl (1988) in her study of Indian household observes that television not only brings orderliness, it brings great disorder to some aspects of life. Television viewing disrupts the round of household activities, especially cooking, eating and night sleep.

Is the medium of television an agent of social change, reinforcer of the value system or a reflector of the existing social structure? Some scholars opt for a middle position. They are of the opinion that television as a medium serves as a source of normative behaviour patterns as well as of advice in coping with everyday problems (Gerbner, 1958; Rainwater, 1959; Tuchman, 1979). A few scholars are of the opinion that television acts as 'a mirror that society holds up to itself' (Katz et. al., 1981). Golding (1981), on the other hand, opines that television contents are value free and they avoid those issues which are controversial and might provoke change. Other scholars regard television medium as reinforcer of the existing structure and exhibit stereotype notions (Dahlgren, 1981; Press, 1989; Wilson, 1981). It is being realized that information and ideas on their own are seldom sufficient to alter these structures. The effects of television transmission should not be thought of only in terms of the spread of information. One of the more important effects is to gradually alter the cultural climate and to introduce new values in a slow and diffuse way (Hartmann et. al., 1989).

The studies on the effects of television viewing have resulted into a controversy--conceiving of the audience as controlling or controlled, as duped or resistant, as making meanings or receiving them. Schramm et. al., (1961) feel that the term "effect" is misleading because it suggests that television 'does something' to the viewers. The connotation is that television is the actor, the viewers are acted upon. It is they who use television rather than television uses them. Seiter et. al., (1989) caution that television spectatorship is much more complicated than the poles of activity and passivity can accommodate. Television viewing is a complicated social experience where different meanings are made of television contents by different viewers. The controversy over the effects of television viewing has resulted into a different stream of studies in which subjectivity of the viewer has been highlighted.

Television contents are transmitted equally to thousands and even millions of people each day at a given period of time but we cannot say that each recipient would perceive television content in the same manner. Their reactions may vary. What meaning each audience member constructs for each piece of television content depends upon one's socio-economic background. Hence to find out commonality in their meanings we have to go back to the commonality of their background. Wilson (1981) perceives that audiences are selective in their attention to the television content. Further, the viewers, depending upon their interest may watch certain television programmes or may switch off their television sets. The right is vested with the viewer. Lull (1988) is of the opinion that viewers not only make their own interpretations of television programmes, they also construct the situations in which viewing takes place and the ways in which acts of viewing and programme contents are put to use at the time of viewing and in subsequent communication activity.

Similarly, Morley (1989) stresses the role of social factors in the production of meaning from television content; the impact of genre on patterns of viewing and negotiations of meaning and the importance of contextualizing television viewing within the framework of everyday life. Fiske (1989) suggests abandoning altogether the categories of 'text' and 'audience' as separate analytical entities. Instead television watching should be conceived of as a process of meaning production in which the 'text' is merely a substratum from which the viewer may construct various realizations. The freedom of the viewer to make socially pertinent meanings and pleasures out of television is considerable. Fiske cites the study of Tulloch and Moran (1986) where school students in working class and middle class made completely different sense out of a television programme depicting youth unemployment. The issue raised by Fiske is also applicable in the Indian setting. Aghi (1977) found that Doordarshan stimulated an interest in educational programmes among the students of Rajasthan. Shukla and Kumar (1977), however, point out that school children did not learn from such programmes. Sinha (1985) while supporting the findings of Shukla and Kumar contended that not only the students but sometimes even the teachers did not comprehend some of the educational programmes of Doordarshan.

The question whether television medium is an agent of change or reinforcer of status-quo cannot be answered in a general way. To answer the question in a more meaningful way, it must be broken down into more meaningful units, specified with respect to content, type and sector of society, type and area of change and status-quo etc. (Rosengren, 1981). The multitude of studies on the effects of television on human behaviour has restated society's concern with effects. It is generally accepted that media does influence individuals but does so among and through a nexus of mediating factors and influences. Mass media is viewed as a contributory agent but not the sole cause in the process of reinforcing existing conditions or in bringing about change (Jowett and O'Donnell, 1986). Taking a hint from such observation we shall now review the literature on effects of television viewing on family and children.

**Television and Family**

To find out the impact of television viewing on intra and inter-family interaction patterns a number of studies have been conducted. Roy (1963) reported that television viewing served as a catalyst of change in two ways: "(i) It offers an opportunity for parents to explore with youngsters, the social and emotional aspects of variety of human experiences and (ii) for many parents it offers new insights into personalities of their children." Television watching reduces boredom and loneliness; however it is not treated as an individual activity but a family activity because in India television viewing is a family affair. Through its entertaining and informative programmes,television brings family members together. Television contents provide subject matter to talk, to discuss and facilitates greater interaction among the household members (Brody et. al., 1983; Goodman, 1983; Lull, 1980).

A number of studies indicate negative effects of television viewing. A study conducted in Israel indicates that primary activity of the people on Friday evening, prior to the introduction of television, was visiting and hosting friends. After the television, social framework of Friday evening has been maintained but the primary content of the visit has changed from conversation to watching television programmes (Gurevitch, 1971). Other scholars observe that family life changed after the first television set has been bought. Introudction of television in the household reduced conversations between married couples (Noelle-Neumann, 1981; Robinson, 1972; Szalai, 1972). Similar was the observation of Comstock (1978) who emphasized that television has reduced interaction between family members. Various researchers on the other hand found social isolation, failure to achieve social integration and lack of social interaction leads to high television viewing (Austin, 1985; Johnstone, 1974; Rosengren and Windahl, 1972).

There is a third set of studies in which television viewing was treated as an event that could encourage or discourage social interaction both inside and outside the household. However, in these studies the actor was the viewer not television. According to Dorr, "television can be used to avoid social interaction by retreating to a place where it is possible to watch television alone or by becoming absorbed enough in television to shut other people out or by requiring other people to be quiet so that the programme can be enjoyed. Alternatively, television viewing can be a shared activity in which the members find the opportunity to talk, to sit close or to be quietly companionable. Even when television viewing is not going on, television can be a stimulus to social interaction" (Dorr, 1986, p. 114).

Rogge (1989) discusses the functions of media use as they are interwoven with a family's need for communication. Based on interviews with hundreds of families in Germany (West) on change in media consumption and changes in the everyday life of the family, Rogge illustrates how changes such as unemployment alter the family's use of and feelings towards television.

When we consider television viewing in the context of household things are quite complicated. In this connection it is important to take note of James Lull's (1982) work. One of the issues which Lull investigates is the question of, "who is responsible for the selection of television programmes at home, how programme selection processes occur and how the roles of family position and family communication patterns influence these activities". Lull's point is that programme selection decisions are often complicated interpersonal communication activities involving intra and inter-family status relations, temporal context, the number of television sets available and role based communication conventions. The central question is of power-relations in the family. Morley (1989) echoed similar expression on television viewing in the domestic context. He opines that one is not able to treat the individual viewer as if he or she were a free or rational consumer in a cultural super market. For many people (and especially for the less powerful members of any household) the programmes they watch are not necessarily programmes which they will have choosen to watch. As soon as one thinks about television in the context of social relations then one is inevitably thinking about television in the context of power relations.

There seems to be two-way relation between mass media and family. Lull (1988) opines that on the one hand television medium is likely to effect family internal dynamics and on the other hand familial social and cultural ethos and norms are likely to influence members television viewing behaviour pattern as well as their interpretations of the programmes.

In the context of family television viewing behaviour pattern, very few studies have been conducted in India. Yadava and Reddi (1988) in their study observe that at the behavioural level, the family undergoes many changes once it acquires a television set. With television at home, frequency of outings in the evening for a move, shopping, strolling in the market or park or visits to neighbours, relatives are substantially reduced. Television is instrumental in keeping the family at home bound in the evening. During occasions of conflict over viewing choices masculine power became evident in the families under study. They further observed that power relations of the family did not undergo changes or they could be observed with regard to handling of television sets. Yadava and Reddi have not indicated whether physical presence of the family members before television encourage or discourage social interactions. With introduction of television, physical proximity may have increased but social togetherness may decrease. Further, television viewing behaviour pattern may be different in the families of different classes. Similarly, sex and age variables of the viewers may influence their motivation for watching different television programmes. Women were found to be more interested in watching entertainment programmes, youth in sports, advertisements attracted children and elderly persons were more interested in information (The Tribune, Sept. 14, 1989).

Some studies have related family's television viewing behaviour pattern with its class background. It is contended that members of lower class watch television for longer duration because its being a cheapest mode of entertainment. The members of the upper classes have alternative sources of entertainment hence are light television viewers. (Bogart, 1962; Greenberg et. al., 1970; Holman and Braithwaite, 1982; Tannis and MacBeth, 1981). In short, meanings and interpretations of television contents are influenced by the class background of the individual as well as the duration for which one is exposed to the stimulus.

**Television and Children**

Children are a special audience group for television transmission. Along with other agents of socialization like family, peer group, play group, teacher etc. television as a medium of commuincation acquaint the children about different things. Its programmes not only educate and entertain the children but also inform and reinforce societal values and norms. The studies conducted on the effects of television viewing on children indicate both positive and negative impacts.

According to Howe (1977) television not only exposes the child to different events and experiences outside his environment but it also exerts influence when the child's knowledge of rules and conventions which govern social actions are incomplete and immature. A number of studies have also revealed that television plays a positive role in children's learning process ( Comstock, 1978; Defleur et. al., 1967; Tannis and MacBeth, 1981). Apart from socialization the young ones, television also helps to resocialize them in terms of imitation of television models and development of child's image of them and then tries to emulate the new social role criteria (Chombart and Jose, 1985).

The commercials on television are specially directed to the children to create a felt need in them. Gorn and Goldberg (1977) are of the view that over exposure to a commercial product produces favourable attitudes towards the advertised product specially among the children. A few studies indicate that failure on the part of parents to buy the advertised product as demanded by their children creates stress in the family. Parents feel that exposure of advertisements to children has increased their demands as it serves as a shopping guide for children. It was found that children develop an inferiority complex if they do not possess a particular advertised product. Refusal to buy things leads to jealousy, isolation followed by tantrums, negative emotions, aggression and misbehaviour (Churchill and George, 1979; Reid and Frazer, 1980; Rossiter and Robertson, 1980; Sharma, 1989).

Television programmes are also associated with negative consequences for the children. Cazeneuve (1964) states that television creates new myths among the children because it has an impact on passive imagination. Persons, world, ideas are presented in a way which mixes fiction and reality. The Senate Sub-committee on Juvenile Delinquency Report with regard to the effects of television commented: "It is clear that television, whose impact on the public mind is equal to or greater than that of any other medium, is a factor in moulding the character, attitudes and behaviour patterns of America's young people" (cited in Larsen, 1968, p. 211). The heavy doses of televised crime, violence and brutality make the children aggressive, disturbed and anguished. This is evidenced by increasing violence in school playgrounds (Churchill, 1981; Halloran et. al., 1970; Heath et. al., 1986; Pourtois, 1978). The aggression may turn into general animosity towards society or into something as a state of mind. It can also lead to maladjustments in taking up adult roles (Malik, 1986).

Parents and social critics are very much aware of television faults. Television introduces children to an adult world they should not yet know about. It is violent, sexist, racist and commercial (Postman, 1982). Opinions about television are very negative. Most respondents perceived the power of television to do harm or to promote mediocrity among their children. They recognized that television contents dispensed misinformation, twisted values and dangerous ideas which were completely devoid of reality (Dorr, 1986).

Dorr is of the opinion that there are broadly two areas of significant debate about the effects of television content on children: "the nature of effects and the characteristics of the affected population. The position one takes in each debate is dependent not only on the available evidence but also on one's model of how television functions in children's lives and it has important implications for one's stance toward and informal regulation of television content" (Dorr, 1986, p. 83).

There is another viewpoint. Scholars are of the opinion that impact of television content, either positive or negative, is not clear particularly in the absence of their background. Comstock (1978) argues that although television appears to function as an agent of socialization yet the degree of its influence is uncertain. In a few studies children's understanding of social interactions shown on television has been examined. It was found that less mature children often imitated the action and dialogue and older children considered the inferential aspects of social interactions (Bearison et. al., 1982; Collins, 1984, Lelfer et. al., 1971; Pingree et. al., 1984). Some scholars have emphasized the importance of social background and duration of exposure. Robert et. al. (1984) while conducting empirical studies for finding out the impact of television on reading habits of children at different grades, came to the conclusion that among other things the socio-economic status of family as well as duration of exposure to television had important role in educational achievement of young television viewers. Ritchie (1987) is also of the view that it is wrong to say that television programmes inculcate reading habits and educational achievement. Instead home environment, individual's commitment to education and time spent on television viewing influence the children's educational achievement rather than television viewing per se.

The review of the studies helps us to conclude that children are the most vulnerable population to be influenced by television watching. However, the impact of television viewing differs according to the class background of the viewers. Hartmann et. al. (1989) in their study in the Indian setting opine: "Information, ideas and values originating in the media acquire currency by the process of diffusion. This process is neither automatic nor indiscriminate; diffusion tends to follow the pattern of social interaction already structured by caste, class, age and sex".

**Theoretical Framework**

During the post-war period audience studies have revolved around "effect" perspective and "uses and gratifications" school. Morley (1989) contends that the history of audience studies oscillates between perspectives which have stressed the power of the text (message/content) over its audiences and perspectives which have stressed the barriers 'protecting' the audience from the potential effects of the message.

**Effect Theory**

The first position is most obviously represented by the whole tradition of effects studies in which media are seen as having the power to "inject" their audiences with particular messages which will cause them to behave in a particular way. One finds curious contradictions in this approach. Television is accused of reducing its audience to the status of "glossy-eyed dupes" who consume a constant diet of predigested junk food, churned out by the media "sausage factory" who suffer the anaesthetic effects of this addictive and narcotic substance (Morley, 1989). Television has also been accused of making us do all manner of things, most notably in the debates around television and violence, where it has been argued that the viewing of violent television programmes will cause the viewers to go out and commit violent acts (Root, 1986). It is a theory about what television does to other, more vulnerable people.

**Uses and Gratification Perspective**

The second key perspective has been the work that has developed principally from the "uses and gratification" school. According to this perspective, the viewer is credited with an active role and it is then a question, of looking at what people do with the media rather than what media do to them (Halloran et. al., 1970). The uses and gratification perspective does represent a significant advance on effects theory as it opens up the question of differential interpretation. This argument was of great significance in moving the debate forward—to begin to look at the active engagement of the audience with the medium and with the particular television programmes that they might be watching (Morley, 1989). From this perspective one can no longer talk about the "effects" of message on a homogeneous mass audience who are expected to be affected in the same manner. However, the limitation is that the "uses and gratifications" perspective remains individualistic in so far as differences of response or interpretation are ultimately attributed to individual differences of personality or psyschology. It is severely limited by its insufficiently sociological or cultural perspective in so far as everything is reduced to the level of variations in individual psychology. Fiske (1989) is of the opinion that watching television is a process of making meaning and pleasure and this process is determined by two parallel and interlocking sets of forces: the social and the textual, the one working upon the subjectivity of the viewer, the other upon the textuality of television. He further suggests abandoning the categories of text and audience as separate analytical entities. Because of the openness of the televisual text and the diversity of patterns of engagement on the part of the viewer, the process of watching television precludes theoretical fixation and can only be approached in terms of moments in the semiotic process, where textual and social lines of force intersect.

**Encoding/Decoding Model**

Stuart Hall's encoding/decoding model of communication was developed as an attempt to take forward insights which has emerged within each of these perspectives (Hall,1980). It took from the effect theorists, the notion that mass communication is a structured activity, in which institutions which produce the message do have a power to set agendas and to define issues. The model also attempted to incorporate, from the uses and gratifications perspective, the model of the active viewer making meaning from the signs and symbols which the media provide. In short, the encoding/decoding model was designed to provide a synthesis of insights that have come out of a series of different perspectives—Communication Theory, Semiology, Sociology and Psychology—and to provide an overall mode of communication circuit as it operated in its social context ( Morley, 1989). However it remains a limited model, in so far as it simply provides for the three logical possibilities of the receiver either sharing, partly sharing or not sharing the code in which the message is sent and therefore, to that extent, being likely to make a dominant, negotiated or oppositional decoding of the encoded message (Bourdieu, 1984). Further, what about the role of television viewer who has the right to watch a programme or to switch off the television set?

Recently a number of shortcomings with the encoding/decoding model of communication have been identified. The concept of the preferred reading, which is of course central to the encoding/decoding model, has been subjected to a number of criticisms. At one level one can ask how specific the concept of preferred reading is to the field of news and current affairs television (within which the encoding/decoding model was first applied). How one might effectively transfer that model to the analysis of fictional television content remains a problem. There are also problems about the exact status of the "preferred reading". Is it something which is in the text or is it something which can be generated from the text by certain methods of semiological analysis, or is it a statement by the analyst, as to how most members of the audience will empirically read a given programme or message (Morley, 1989; Wren-Lewis, 1983).

If we are to theorize the subject of television, it has to be theorized in its cultural and historical specificity. As most of the studies noted above were conducted in other countries where television transmission is not under the complete control of government, their methodologies and results are not applicable to the Indian setting. Unfortunately very few studies have been conducted in India where the impact of television viewing on children and family dynamics has been studied. We are still at a point where much knowledge is anecdotal and a few studies, which have been conducted in India have very limited empirical base, it was decided not to make use of any theoretical framework. However an attempt will be made to test the reciprocal hypothesis, that is, television programmes influence the viewers differently according to their socio-economic background. In other words, members of different classes perceive different meanings from the same television programme.

**Objectives of Study**

The present study is motivated by two-fold objectives: First, to find out the extent to which television viewing has brought about changes in attitudes and behaviour pattern of the viewers, and second, to explicate the differential impact of television watching on the viewers. To find out the effects of television viewing the study is confined to intra and inter-family network of relations as well as on the children with different class background. Reactions of the viewers were sought whether they were in favour of granting autonomy to television or wanted to retain the status quo, that is, retaining State control over television in India. Further, their views regarding the impact of cable network programmes on their children as well as comparison with that of programmes of Doordarshan were sought.

To attain the above noted main aims the study attempts to answer the following specific research questions :

1. Does the family television viewing behaviour pattern vary according to the class background of the viewers?
2. Do the motivations for watching and interpretations of television programmes are related with age, sex and class background of the television viewers?
3. Do the perceived effects of television viewing associated with their class background?
4. In which way family power relations become evident with regard to choice of television programmes, handling of television set or VCR / VCP and buying of advertized goods etc?
5. To what extent television watching facilitates or hinders social interactions within and outside the family?
6. How do the parents perceive their children's television viewing behaviour pattern? What time children spend on television watching do they make some adjustments in their routines to watch television? In what manner parents control and regulate their children's television viewing?
7. What motivates the children to watch television programmes? Are they more interested in entertainment programmes as compared with educative and

informative programmes? To what extent television commercials create felt need in the children and how they persuade their parents to buy those items?

8. Do the parents perceive positive or negative effects of television watching on their children? What remedial steps they take?

9. To what extent duration, motivations and effects of television watching on children are associated with the class background of their families?

10. To what extent Doordarshan programmes have created an awareness among the viewers regarding different social problems of our country? How viewers of different class background perceive and interpret these programmes?

11. Do the viewers perceive that Doordarshan programmes disseminate correct or twisted information? To what extent governmental professed objectives of television in India have been achieved? Do the meanings and interpretations of television contents differ according to the class background of the viewers?

12. How do the viewers evaluate the functioning of Doordarshan transmission in India? Are the viewers in favour of granting autonomy to Doordarshan or are they interested in retaining the status quo, that is, Government control over television transmission?

13. What motivated respondents to have cable television connection and how they evaluate transmission from cable television vis-a-vis Doordarshan as well as impact of cable transmission on their children?

**Where and how the study was conducted**

The study was conducted at Chandigarh which has a population of approximately six lakhs (0.6 million). The city is one of the few planned cities of India and is divided into different sectors. The city at the present serves as a capital for the States of Punjab and Haryana as well as of Union Territory of Chandigarh.The housing pattern is clearly demarcated ranging from one room set to large bungalow type. The households possessing television sets at Chandigarh were treated as a universe for the present study.

**Sampling**

The main objective of the study was to find out the impact of television viewing across different segments of Chandigarh population. Exposure to television programmes was treated as an intervening variable which was dependent upon socio-economic status of the viewers, which in turn influenced their attitudes and behaviour patterns. Hartmann et. al. (1989) concludes that studies are apt to show that media exposure is dependent upon such things as education and income but attitudes and practices are to some extent related to media consumption. To attain the objective of the study it was decided to give equal representation to three broad social classes, that is, upper, middle and lower.

We were aware of the fact that population of Chandigarh was of pyramid type. A few persons occupy the top position and a large population is placed at the bottom. However, taking into consideration the possession of television sets the distribution is of reverse order, that is, a few households from the lower class possess television sets and almost all persons of upper class have one or more television sets. Hence for the purpose of comparison it was decided to go for a purposive sample of 100 households in each class who possessed at least one television set.

We were then confronted with the problem of identifying people belonging to different classes. Clear-cut housing pattern of Chandigarh came to our rescue. As a preliminary step it was decided to divide the households into three categories depending upon the house type. One and two room apartments were designated as lower type, three and four room sets were treated as middle category and houses with five or more rooms were labelled as higher type. However, to place them into social classes variables of education, occupation and income were considered and the respondents were redistributed. There was no difficulty in identifying the households possessing television sets because to attain clear reception of television transmission persons possessing television sets had installed tall antenna at their houses. In this manner viewers were identified based on their house type and possession of television sets in different sectors of Chandigarh. However, only those viewers were to be included in the sample who were living with their children. This was done to put a check on the bias of the researchers as well as to get meaningful reactions of the viewers regarding their children's television viewing behaviour pattern. In all we had 300 cases from different sectors representing three house types, that is, 100 cases from each house type.

### Technique of Data Collection

Taking into account the specific objectives of the study an interview schedule was constructed. After pretesting ten cases from each house type necessary modifications were made. The interview schedule used had both open and close ended questions. First part of the schedule included questions to know the socio-economic and demographic characteristics of the respondents. Second section dealt with their television viewing behaviour pattern, duration of time spent on television viewing, modifications made in their household and other activities, programmes liked most, perceived effects of television watching on the internal dynamics of family relations as well as on inter family social interactions and their interpretations of the television programmes. Their reactions were also sought with regard to commercials shown on television and their impact on their household buying practices. The third section was earmarked to find out children's television viewing behaviour pattern, motivations for such watching and perceived consequences thereof. They were also asked about the mechanism adopted to control and regulate their children's television viewing behaviour. The last section was divided into two parts. Part one had questions pertaining to different social issues of Indian society and how the viewers were made aware about them by watching different television programmes. They were also asked to indicate the nature of change that took place in their attitudes and behaviour after being exposed to television contents. The exercise was done to get a feedback from the viewers about the professed functions of television in India. The other part was meant to find out the reactions of the viewers. Were they satisfied with the present system, that is, State control over television transmission or the viewers felt that television contents were twisted and did not disseminate correct information and they wanted to grant autonomy to television. Further they were asked to compare Doordarshan programmes vis-a-vis cable television transmission. In short, for the purpose of collecting core data for the study an interview schedule was used.

In addition to interview schedule, observation as a technique of data collection was also used, particularly with regard to their sitting arrangements for television watching and other behaviour pattern when the programmes were on. Secondary data pertaining to the growth of television in India was also made use of to highlight the issue that television as a medium of mass communication is quite recent one. The techniquè of content analysis was used to find out the time which commercials consumed during television serial etc. In short, to supplement the core data collected with the help of an interview schedule, other techniques were also used. The core data was collected during a time of nine months that is, from February 1991 to October 1991.

## Unit of Study

Television watching is treated as a family activity rather than an individual activity because only a few families possess two or more television sets in their houses. Instead of interviewing each and every member of the household it was decided to treat woman in the house as a unit of study. It was done for a number of reasons: (i) we did not evolve any objective method to measure the effects of television viewing but took into account only the perceived effects. Hence women respondents were thought to be better equipped with information pertaining to changes in intra and inter-family social interactions; (ii) we were also interested to know the effects of television viewing on the children in the family and respondents being mothers could give their perception in a more candid manner; and (iii) their availability which was essential to collect primary data. As a majority of the women were not expected to be engaged in paid work it was easier to contact them for their responses.

With regard to present age of the respondents 68 per cent were in the middle age group, that is, 30-45 years. The younger (up to 30 years) and older (45 years and above) age groups were 15.33 per cent and 16.67 per cent respectively. The low representation of the respondents in the younger and older age groups was attributed to the fact that we selected the sample of those respondents who were living with their children. The respondents of the younger age who did not have children and older respondents whose children were living away from them were not included in the sample. It was due to this reason that we had a higher representation of the respondents of the middle age.

For the purpose of determining the class background of the respondents we took into account the income, occupation and education of their husband because a majority of the respondents were not engaged in any paid work. The association between income, occupation and education was worked out with the help of gamma test. The value of gamma in case of income and occupation was 0.86; income and education it was 0.81 and for education and occupation its value was 0.81 (The formation in tabular form has been given in Appendix 'A').

After having established high association between income, occupation and education we could have taken up class background of the respondent's husband based on any one of the variables. But to ward off a few discrepancies, that is, persons with high income not having high education or being engaged in occupation of high prestige, a comprehensive index was worked out. The score of one on each variable was given to those persons who had low income, education and occupation. On the other end, heads who had high income, engaged in occupations of high prestige and with high education were given the score of three on each variable. The scores of each person could range between 3 to 9 on all the three variables taken together.

The scores of the husbands residing in small houses ranged between three to six. In the case of those residing in medium type of houses their scores ranged between 3 to 9 whereas those residing in bigger houses scored between 5 to 9. Taking into account the scores of the husbands it was decided to treat persons with score of 3 and 4 as belonging to the lower class. We had 80 such persons living in small houses and 20 living in medium size houses. After combining them we had 100 persons who contituted the lower class. For considering the upper class it was decided that only those persons who scored between 8 and 9 would be considered. There were 52 persons who were residing in large house and 10 persons were living in medium size houses but had the score of 8 & 9. Those who scored 8 and 9 their number came to 62 and they were treated as belonging to the upper class. So far as the middle category was concerned we had representation from all the three type of houses and their score ranged from 5 to 7 and there were 138 cases who constituted the middle class.

On the basis of the scores on all the three variables the husbands of the respondents were grouped into three social classes and the sample was redistributed. Out of 300 respondents 100 were treated as belonging to the lower class, 138 to the middle class and 62 to the upper class.

In our subsequent analysis social class was treated as an independent variable to find out the impact of television viewing. We were of the opinion that the impact of television watching and interpretation of television programmes would be perceived differently by the members of different social classes. It, however, did not imply that television content had no impact on television viewers but we felt that impact of television viewing would be qualitatively different among the members of different social classes.

# 2
# Families Watch Television

Since the turn of the last century a wide variety of researches have been attempted to understand the significance of family. These researches give scholarly accounts of the family and range from death of the family to family passing through golden era. But even the most recent accounts exclude considerations of the mass-media or treat them only as an aside in their description of family life. To media scholars this may seem to be an obvious oversight in need of correction (Lull, 1988). Research on television viewing has generally excluded indepth treatment of the family which is the natural viewing group. Television viewing is not an isolated individual activity in India, but watching television is a family activity that involves an intermeshing of the constantly changing personal agendas, moods and emotional priorities of each family member with the fluctuating agenda of programmes that emanates from the television sets. This does not mean that we cannot generalize about patterns, that is, normative style of viewing which are evident in individual family and across families. We must however, keep in mind that these are highly complex and dynamic patterns (Lull, 1988).

To find out the impact of television viewing on family,the chapter has been divided into two sections. The first section analyses the consequences of introduction of television set on the internal dynamics of family relations. In which way television viewing alters the routine of the family members or brings the family members together, provides them subject matter to talk so that they have greater interaction among themselves. The second section will take into account social interactions outside the family. An attempt will be made to find out the extent to which introduction of television set in the family has facilitated or hindered social interactions with neighbours and other activities of the members outside their families.

Television transmission is, no doubt, one way communication. Nevertheless, viewers not only make their interpretations of the programmes but they also construct the situations in which acts of viewing and programme contents are put to use at the time of viewing and in subsequent communication activity. Thus, one cannot take family viewing for granted. There seems to be two way relation between television and family. On the one hand television transmission is likely to affect family internal and external network of relations and on the other hand, familial social and cultural ethos are likely to influence television viewing behaviour pattern as well as interpretations of the programmes. In this chapter on family television viewing, we are mainly concerned with the qualitative character of the relationship i.e., how television programmes influence the family and how family interprets and uses television within its social and cultural context.

**Section A**

For the sake of analysis and clarity the first section of the chapter has been further divided into (i) Family television viewing style; (ii) Motivation for television viewing; and (iii) Consequences of television viewing on the families. Under the sub-head of family television viewing style,an attempt will be made to identify the location of television sets in the houses of the respondents of different classes, the duration of time since when they were possessing television sets, their number and type as well as possession of VCR/VCP, connection of cable network and the time spent on television watching. It is assumed that family television viewing styles are dependent on the class background of the television owners. Though television transmits the same content at a given period of time yet people with different class backgrounds are likely to perceive the programme contents differently. Such an assumption will be examined under the sub-head of motivation for television viewing. In the last section, the consequences of television viewing on the internal dynamics of the families of the respondents will be identified. Whether the respondents associate positive or negative consequences and how the respondents of different classes perceive the consequences. It may be added here that we have not evolved any objective criteria to identify changes to be associated with the introduction of television set in the family but we have relied upon the respondents and their perception regarding effects of television viewing on their families.

**(i) Family Television Viewing Style**

Television has been called as a member of the family

(Singer and Singer, 1977). Since no other member of the family commands direct attention than television for a substantial period of time. Television set is to be located at a convenient and at conspicuous place where family members could easily sit and watch television transmission.

Television sets in the houses of the respondents belonging to the lower class were normally placed at a conspicuous place. In the one room house television set was placed on a well decorated rack of the main wall of the house or placed on the shelf. The television sets were found covered with decorated covers. In this way, television not only got a place of importance in the house but it also became a status symbol for the family.The television sets were placed in the rooms in such a manner that the members of the family and their neighbours could sit on the floor or on the cot, so that they could view the programmes. Children were normally asked to sit on the floor and the elders either sat on the chairs or on the cot.

Television sets in the houses of the middle class were found to be invariably placed in the drawing/living rooms and in a few cases in the bedrooms. Television sets were either placed on a table or in a cabinet like structure and were placed in one corner, so that members could sit on chairs/sofa set or beds to watch the programmes. The nearest chair/sofa from the set was normally found at the minimum distance of 4 to 5 feet. No particular sitting arrangement for different members of family was noticed in their houses. In those houses which had two television sets, one television set was found in the bedroom of the head of the household.

In the houses of the respondents of the upper class television sets were found to be in the drawing/living rooms and/or bedrooms.The television set placed in drawing/living room was generally found to be lying in a cabinet or on a trolly and was placed in a corner so that people sitting on sofa could easily watch the programmes. Here again, we did not find any distinction with regard to the sitting arrangement of the members of the family. However, in a few families television sets were also found in the bedrooms of the children in addition to the bedroom of the conjugal unit.

It was around 1982 when coloured television sets were made freely available. The change in the technology pushed up the sale of the television sets. Moreover, the organisation of the Asiad Games in India was responsible for mad rush for buying coloured television sets. Those families who had earlier black and white television sets disposed off their old sets and bought new coloured television sets. There were a number of enterprising television companies which also offered replacement of black and white television with coloured television sets with some additional money. The members belonging to lower class took advantage of such a situation and bought black and white television sets.

Tabulation of data pertaining to the period since the respondents were possessing television set class-wise indicated that a majority (91.93 per cent) of the respondents of the upper class had been possessing television sets for the last 10 years and more. Similarly more than 74 per cent of the respondents belonging to the middle class had bought television sets during the period and only 35 per cent respondents of the lower class had bought television sets during that period. We notice a progressive decrease in the percentages of the respondents if we move from upper through middle to lower class while taking into account the period of possession of television sets as ten years and more.

The respondents were further asked whether they possessed colour television and if yes, since how long. It was noted that approximately 80 per cent of the respondents of the upper class, 65 per cent of the middle class and 20 per cent of the lower class had colour television sets and most of them bought these sets during the last ten years or earlier. The respondents were further asked, whether they had two or more television sets, it was noted that not a single household from the lower class had 2 or more television sets. However, in constrast to 18 per cent households of the middle class, 32 per cent households of the upper class had 2 or more television sets at their houses. Similar pattern was also noticed with regard to posession of VCR/VCP. In the case of the upper class 64 per cent of them had VCR/VCP, 42 per cent of the middle class and only 10 per cent respondents of the lower class possessed VCR/VCP. From early 1991 transmission from cable television was made available in a few sectors at Chandigarh. Particularly after the Gulf War and with the accessibility of a number of channels people of upper and middle classes had gone for it. Among the respondents of upper and middle classes 35 per cent and 27 per cent respectively had cable television connections and only five respondents of the lower class had access to cable networks. These respondents were asked to indicate the motivations for seeking links to cable networks because at Chandigarh such links would cost Rs. 200/-p.m.The respondents informed us that they did not find Doordarshan programmes interesting and it is for variety and entertainment that they would not mind paying extra money every month. It is due to uninteresting Doordarshan programmes and for having a choice for additional channels that these respondents have gone for cable networks. A few respondents of the middle and upper classes had gone for cable networks because they could see Hindi and English movies daily. The class distinction becomes quite obvious with regard to possession of colour television sets, possessing 2 or more television sets, VCR/VCPs and cable television connection.

In the initial stages when the family acquires a television set, it has novelty value and all the members watch programmes as often as possible. Soon the novelty aspect wears off and television watching is reduced (Yadava and Reddy, 1988). There are a few studies which have tried to find out association between social class and time spent on television viewing. It is generally believed that members of the lower class spend more time on television viewing, because it is the cheapest mode of entertainment (Dorr, 1986). Let us find out the time spent on television viewing by members belonging to different classes.

TABLE 2.1: Distribution according to the time spent on television viewing

| Time spent | Classes | | | Total |
|---|---|---|---|---|
| | Upper | Middle | Lower | |
| Up to 1 hour | 18 (29.03) | 30 (21.74) | 12 (12.00) | 60 (20.00) |
| 1-3 hours | 35 (56.45) | 72 (52.17) | 50 (50.00) | 157 (52.34) |
| 3-5 hours | 9 (14.52) | 35 (25.36) | 32 (32.00) | 76 (25.33) |
| 5+ | | 1 (0.73) | 6 (6.00) | 7 (2.33) |
| Total | 62 (100.00) | 138 (100.00) | 100 (100.00) | 300 (100.00) |

Television viewing is not an individual affair but is a family activity. Members of the household watch some programmes collectively and depending upon the time available to them as well as their interest. Some members may continuously watch television programmes, while others may watch for sometime and in between attend to other activities. It is difficult to apportion time budgeting for each member of the household, yet an attempt was made to ask the respondents, how much time on an average the family members spent daily on television viewing. Similar question was also asked regarding viewing time of their husbands.

Viewing time was calculated according to the class background of the respondents and it was noted that only 14.52 per cent respondents of the upper class watched television programmes on an average of 3 hours or more daily. In case of the middle class this percentage increased to 26.09 per cent and it further increased to 38 per cent for the respondents of the lower class. The tabulation helps us to conclude that members of the lower class watch television programmes for a longer duration as compared with members of upper and middle classes. Conversely we noted that those respondents who watched television programmes on an average for an hour daily, there was progressive increase in the percentage of the respondents if we moved from the lower class through the middle to the upper class respondents. In the case of respondents of the lower class 12 per cent watched television programmes for an hour. Out of the respondents of the middle class 21.74 per cent watched for that duration and 29.03 per cent respondents of the upper class spent on average one hour on television viewing. It may, however, be added that more than 52.34 per cent of our respondents belonging to all the classes watched television programmes from 1 to 3 hours daily.

As most of the working male members of the household were expected to be on the work site and were likely to be engaged in number of other activities, they were expected to spend less time on television viewing as compared with their wives.

The husbands of the respondents of the upper class spent less time on watching television programmes as compared with their counterparts of the middle and lower classes. In case of the upper class 75.81 per cent husbands of the respondents spent on an average less than one hour on television viewing, whereas this percentage was reduced to 37.23 per cent in case of the middle class and was further reduced to 20.83 per cent in case of the lower class. Conversely if we take into account the time spent on television viewing from 3-5 hours daily we notice that there is a progressive increase in percentage if we move from upper to lower classes. In case of husbands of the respondents of the upper classes only 3.22 per cent spent on an average 3-5 hours on television viewing. For the middle class this percentage came to 14.59 per cent and for the lower class it further increased to 25.00 per cent.

Keeping in view the television watching time of the respondents belonging to different classes as well as their husbands, we noted that members belonging to the upper class on an average spent less time on television viewing as compared with members of the lower class. We also noted that there was a difference in viewing time between sexes. The male members on an average spent less time on television viewing as compared with women (respondents).

There is one hour programme in the afternoon i.e. 2.00 to 3.00 p.m. which is designed for household ladies who are normally available during this period and this is more true in case of non-working respondents. The respondents were asked, whether they generally watched afternoon Doordarshan programme which was women oriented. We were interested to know not only the percentage distribution of the afternoon viewers according to their class background but also the motivation for viewing such programmes. It may, however, be added that we had 129 women engaged in paid work in our sample and they were not likely to be available at the time when the afternoon Doordarshan transmission was available, with the exception of those whose working time was quite elastic that they were free during the afternoon transmission.

**TABLE 2.2: Distribution of respondents class-wise according to their watching of afternoon Doordarshan transmission**

| Afternoon Watching | Upper | Classes Middle | Lower | Total |
|---|---|---|---|---|
| Yes | 20 (32.26) | 71 (51.45) | 35 (35.00) | 126 (42.00) |
| No | 42 (67.74) | 67 (48.55) | 65 (65.00) | 174 (58.00) |
| Total | 62 (100.00) | 138 (100.00) | 100 (100.00) | 300 (100.00) |

Afternoon Television viewing by the respondents is, no doubt, dependent upon a number of factors, yet it was noted that more women respondents of the middle class watched Doordarshan afternoon transmission in contrast to the upper and lower classes. In case of the middle class 51.45 per cent women respondents normally watched afternoon Doordarshan transmission whereas 32.26 per cent of the upper class and 35 per cent respondents of the lower class watched afternoon transmission. No doubt, the percentage of afternoon viewers of the upper and lower classes approximate to each other, we expected that the motivations for watching afternoon Doordarshan television programme were different according to their class background.

When the respondents specified the motivations for afternoon Doordarshan viewing, we noted that the respondents of the upper class watched Doordarshan programmes for knowing about different recipes, household decoration, embroidery, women's career and entertainment in that order. In the case of women of the lower class the motivations for afternoon television viewing was mainly entertainment followed by knowing about home-made cures, child care and embroidery work. For the respondents of the middle class, afternoon transmission was meant for knowing about different recipes, entertainment, household care and home-made cures. Taking into account the motivating factors for afternoon Doordarshan programme viewing, it becomes obvious that the respondents belonging to different classses viewed television programme for different reasons, implying thereby that class background played an important role in determining their motivations.

The respondents who watched afternoon Doordarshan transmission were further asked whether their husbands also watched such programmes alongwith them. An insignificant number of respondents, 4 from the upper class, 10 from the middle class and 8 from the lower class admitted that when their husbands were at home during the period of afternoon Doordarshan transmission, they also watched women oriented programmes simply to give company to them. Those respondents who had access to cable networks watched transmission of cable television rather than viewing Doordarshan programmes during day time. It was further revealed that women put the television on, and continued to perform different household activities.

It may, however, be added that with the exception of afternoon Doordarshan transmission which is women oriented or UGC programmes which are educational programmes for the students of 8 to 10 classes,other programmes of Doordarshan are generally meant for all the members of the family. The programmes of Doordarshan at the prime time i.e. from 9.00 p.m. to 9.30 p.m. and Sunday programmes are generally viewed by all the members of the family together provided they are liked by them. Our respondents informed us that almost all the family members religiously watched the epic story of Mahabharat when it was shown on Doordarshan.

We also enquired from the respondents about the normal time when they switched on their television sets. This exercise was done for two reasons: (i) to find out whether television viewing is family activity or an individual activity; and (ii) to explicate the power dynamics of the family.

The information thus collected indicated that most of the families switched on their television sets in the evening. In case of the members of the lower class they switched on television sets as and when their menfolk returned home from work. It was only in few cases where women put the television on as soon as the evening session of Doordarshan started. So far as the middle and upper classes were concerned they put the television on according to the programmes they wanted to watch irrespective whether their menfolk were at home or not. It was more true in those cases who had access to channels of cable transmission. The respondents of the upper and middle classes further informed that their children were knowledgeable about programmes and the handling of television set particularly with regard to adjustment of colour, brightness of the image etc. Among the lower class the children were not permitted to handle the television sets. In the evening particularly during the serials of Doordarshan all the family members watched television programmes together. Similar was the case with regard to movies and other entertaining programmes. We were further informed by our respondents, who owned VCR/VCP and had access to cable transmission that instead of viewing uninterested Doordarshan programmes they used VCR/VCP, or cable networks to watch programmes of their interests. It was interesting to note that women respondents admitted that they had no knowledge about the technical mechanism of handling VCR/VCP. Further, when all the family members watched television programmes or used VCR/VCP, the remote control usually remained in the hands of their husbands or grown up children. The respondents of upper and middle classes, who were having facility of cable transmission, also revealed that their children watched programmes of cable network whenever they had free time and would switch on a particular channel of their choice.

Hence it can be concluded that the family television viewing style differed from one class to another and with the exception of few programmes, television viewing was not an individual activity among the members of lower class but was a family activity. Further male members had control over handling of television, and VCR/VCP. However, in the case of respondents who had access to cable networks or owned VCR/VCP, television watching was an individual activity depending upon their interests and liking.

**(ii) Motivations for Television Viewing**

In the preceding analysis it was observed that television viewing behaviour pattern of the respondents was related to their class background and television viewing was generally a family activity. We are now interested to find out the degree to which family and class background of the respondents influence their choice of certain programmes as well as the motivation for selection.

We assume that selection of the programmes and motivation for viewing Doordarshan programmes are also class oriented. To examine such an assumption, different Doordarshan programmes were grouped under broad categories of serials, entertainment, informative and educative programmes. Under each broad head different programmes shown on Doordarshan were indicated to find out differential selection of these programmes by the members of different classes. It will not be out of the context to mention here that different programmes are likely to be watched by members of the family together. There would, however, be certain programmes in which some members would show greater interest as compared with other members of the family. The television set would be on and some members would occasionally watch these programmes if they did not have any other activity to do. Television viewing as a family activity became a common feature during serials shown at the prime time as well as on Sundays or when the movie or chitrahaars were shown on the television. It is for the convenience that we have asked the respondents about the different programmes which were watched by the family members rather than asking each and every member of the household.

The enlistment of different programmes watched by the members indicated that with the exception of watching Ramayana andMahabharathashown on Doordarshan, there was marked difference in the selection of programmes by the families of different classes. The motivating factors for the families of the upper class to watch Ramayana and Mahabharatha were for the sake of knowing history, mythology and old traditions. The members of the middle class viewed them because they depicted great past of Indian history, mythology as well as for the sake of religiosity. In case of the members of the lower class, they watched Ramayana and Mahabharatha for knowing the mythology in the right perspective, religiosity and for entertainment. With regard to other serials shown at the prime time, it was observed that members of the lower class followed by the middle and upper classes viewed these serials regularly for entertainment and to pass time. We also found marked difference in the selection of women oriented programmes according to the class background of the respondents. Further, the families which had access to cable networks watched transmission from these channels if they did not like some serials of Doordarshan or switched off the television.

Entertainment seems to be the major motivating factor for the members of the lower class to watch television programmes. This becomes obvious, if we look at the proportion of the respondents belonging to different classes, who watched movies and chitrahaars (songs from films) and regional songs and dances shown on Doordarshan. Classical Indian music and dances as well as Western music were found to be more popular among the upper segments of our respondents as and when they were beamed on Doordarshan.

Under the informative programmes with the exception

of Doordarshan news, we noticed class differences in the selection of different informative programmes. More members of the upper and middle classes watched quiz, focus, current affairs and programmes related to science and technology and very few members from the lower class were attracted to these programmes. The difference according to the class background of the members may be attributed to the language of such programmes. So far as the Doordarshan news are concerned they are telecast in regional languages, Hindi and English and people could watch according to their comprehension. In the case of other informative programmes they were not very popular among the lower segments because these programmes were generally telecast in English. Most of the respondents, who had connection for cable networks, also used BBC channel for news. They told us that news on Doordarshan were not informative. The contents referred to the statements of Ministers or the leaders of the opposition. When the parliament session was on there would be news in Hindi followed by 'Sansad Samachar', news in English and then 'Parliament news' which were simply repetitions.

Among the different educational programmes being telecast on Doordarshan, it was noted that those programmes were not very popular among the viewers. Certain programmes pertaining to health awareness, literacy promotion and dealing with the legal cases were relatively popular among the lower class. As members of the upper and middle classes were found to be more educated,they were quite aware about the contents, thus showed indifference. However, programmes which shower light on history were found to be popular among the upper classes.

Selection of different programmes by the members of different social class background, further supports our contention that all the programmes shown on Doordarshan are not uniformly watched by the viewers but keeping in view their class background the viewers were found to be selective. There were two exceptions, i.e., the serials of Ramayana and Mahabharatha and Doordarshan news which were watched by most of the people irrespective of their class background, yet their motivations for watching these programmes were different.

The less proportion of the members of the upper class who used Doordarshan as a source of entertainment as compared with members of lower class, does not imply that television is not used by the upper segments for entertainment. In case certain programmes on television do not come up to the expectations of the people and who have alternative sources like cable TV or VCR/VCP, they would prefer to use such alternatives instead of depending upon 'enforced viewing'. It may be added here that television in India is State controlled and viewers in Chandigarh can watch programmes of Jalandhar and Delhi Kendras of Doordarshan. Further after 8.40 p.m. the regional centre of Jalandhar is hooked up with the National Programme and programmes of Delhi Doordarshan are only shown. The respondents of the upper and middle classes were very much annoyed with the programmes of Doordarshan. They informed us that the quality of the programmes of Doordarshan had gone down. Even the serials shown during the prime time, that is, 9.00 p.m. to 9.30 p.m. and on Sundays were not interesting. Due to lack of variety and uninteresting programmes of Doordarshan they would like to go for cable networks as and when such facility is available in their sectors. A few members of the lower class who owned VCR/VCP also used it for viewing Hindi movies for their entertainment. A few families of the lower class used their VCR/VCP for commercial purposes also, that is, they showed Hindi movies and charged a nominal fee from the viewers or gave it on rental basis. However, a good proportion of members of the middle class and 90 per cent of the lower class, who did not own VCR/VCP or cable television had to depend upon Doordarshan transmission. Hence in the absence of other alternatives, television watching was an 'enforced viewing' for them unless they switched off the television during the programmes which were not according to their liking. The members of the upper and middle classes used their VCR/VCP and cable networks to watch programmes of their own choice rather than depending on programmes of Doordarshan.

Television is India was made commercial in January 1976. Television is called commercial when the cost of production and broadcasting as well as profits are derived from advertising revenue. Most people would not buy television sets simply to watch commercials. Interesting and entertaining programmes are created and sponsored by commercial houses so that people are attracted to see these programmes and it is through these shows that advertisement agencies put up their products. William Melody (1973) astutely observed that the programmes are the bait used to lure the viewers into a position where they can be exposed to persuasive messages. Les Brown (1971) succinctly stated that advertiser bought audience not programmes. Since Indian television has become commercial, there is a debate going on about the time allocation for the commercials to be shown on television. Government of India has claimed that out of the total telecast time only 2.5 per cent time was allocated to the advertising houses. However, the commercials are concentrated on the prime time as well as during the most popular serial or other programme. During the telecast of Mahabharatha serial which was officially announced to be telecast from 10 to 11 a.m. the commercials were shown for 25 minutes and the serial was shown only for 35 minutes out of the allotted one hour. Similar was the situation with regard to other popular programmes of Doordarshan. The respondents who were having access to cable network complained that commercials of the same company are repeated time and again in between the programmes which were very irritating. They opined that Doordarshan was relatively better off in the sense that the commercials were shown in the beginning and these commercials were not placed during the actual programme.

To find out the exposure to commercials the respondents were asked to indicate whether they switched on the television to watch a popular programme at the allocated time. This question was asked to find out their interest in watching commercials because all the viewers were expected to be aware that actual programmes started quite late. It was assumed that members of the lower class who watched television mainly for entertainment would not mind watching the commercials as well. In contrast to this members of the upper class who were expected to be more time conscious were likely to switch on the television approximately at the time when commercials were over.

TABLE 2.3: **Respondents switching on television at the time announced for a particular programme of Doordarshan**

| | Classes | | | |
|---|---|---|---|---|
| Responses | Upper | Middle | Lower | Total |
| Yes | 20<br>(32.25) | 68<br>(49.27) | 82<br>(82.00) | 170<br>(56.66) |
| No | 42<br>(67.75) | 70<br>(50.73) | 18<br>(18.00) | 130<br>(43.34) |
| Total | 62<br>(100.00) | 138<br>(100.00) | 100<br>(100.00) | 300<br>(100.00) |

In response to the question, do you switch on the television to watch a programme at the time announced? The tabulation of the responses indicated a progressive increase in the percentage of those who switched on the television at the time announced if we moved from the upper through middle to the lower class. In case of members of the upper class only 32.26 per cent switched on the television at the allocated time for a popular programme. A majority of the respondents of the upper class did not switch on the televi sion to watch a popular programme at the time announced but at the time when the actual programme started. In contrast to this 82 per cent members of the lower class switched on the television at the time announced. It is obvious from the responses that a majority of members of the upper class were not interested to look at the commercials. In case of members of the middle class they were equally divided i.e. approximately 50 per cent watched commercials as well. On the other hand, 82 per cent of the members of the lower segment watched commercials also because they felt that these commercials provided some entertainment to them.

The above discussion on the selection of television programmes and the motivation for their selection clearly indicates that the class background of the families under study plays an important role not only in the selection of certain programmes but also in their motivations. It was noted that families of the lower class treated television contents as a source of entertainment, whereas members of the middle and upper classes in addition to treating television content as a source of entertainment, used television for informative and educational purposes. Further, the commercials shown on the television have the viewers from the lower and middle classes. It would be interesting to know the extent to which exposure to these commercials have an impact on family's market buying behaviour pattern.

**(iii) Consequences of Television Viewing on Family**

Changes in family structure are not likely to be directly related with the introduction of television sets in Indian homes. Nevertheless, introduction of television is likely to bring about certain changes in the familial interaction as well as behaviour pattern. At the behavioural level the family undergoes changes once it acquires a television set. With television at home, the time spent on outings in the evenings, for movies, shopping etc. are substantially reduced (Yadav and Reddy, 1988). Further the families are likely to make adjustment with regard to time budgeting, preparation of food, eating as well as sleeping behaviour pattern. Television is also likely to facilitate greater interaction between the family members because of their availability at home to watch television programmes. In other words, television is instrumental in keeping the family home bound in the evenings and it provides the cheapest mode of entertainment. In this sub-section of the chapter an attempt is being made to find out the extent to which introduction of television has an impact on the intra familial behaviour pattern.

The respondents were asked, 'whether they have rescheduled their daily chores after buying television'. If yes, in what way? The daily chores here referred to time of preparing food, eating and sleeping. Further, rescheduling also involved their outings in the evenings, shopping, strolling etc.

TABLE 2.4: **Respondents who rescheduled their daily chores**

| | Classes | | | |
|---|---|---|---|---|
| Rescheduling | Upper | Middle | Lower | Total |
| Yes | 32<br>(51.61) | 80<br>(57.97) | 83<br>(83.00) | 195<br>(65.00) |
| No | 30<br>(48.39) | 58<br>(42.03) | 17<br>(17.00) | 105<br>(35.00) |
| Total | 62<br>(100.00) | 138<br>(100.00) | 100<br>(100.00) | 300<br>(100.00) |

The introduction of television sets in houses of the respondents has put some pressure on the families of the respondents to reschedule their daily chores. It is interesting to note that irrespective of social background a majority of the respondents have altered their routines. However, such rescheduling is more prominent in the families of the lower class. In case of respondents of the upper class 51.6 per cent have rescheduled the time at which they had their dinner. In case of the middle class approximately 58 per cent have rescheduled the time of eating and cooking. In contrast to this, 83 per cent families of the lower class have rescheduled their cooking, eating and sleeping behaviour patterns so that these activities did not interfere in their television watching. Introduction of television in their homes have made them time conscious. They looked at the television programmes to know the time and accordingly adjusted their household work.

During the field work for the present study, it was observed that the women of the lower class families either cooked their food before the television was switched on or during the news interval. It was also observed that family members ate their meals before the television and particularly when the News were being telecast. In case of the middle class it was observed that women of the house prepared the meals during the news or intervals and in between the programmes. Members ate their food either during Hindi News or English News, while switching off the television. In case of the members of the upper class who normally had some helping hand in the kitchen, rescheduled their eating habits, that is, they ate after the English News were over or during the serials shown at the prime time, in which they were not interested.

Introduction of television in the family has forced the family members to reschedule their time budgeting. It has made them time conscious and has altered their routine with regard to household work, cooking, eating, sleeping, marketing etc. The respondents perceived that changes had also an adverse effect. The food was cooked in a hurry and eaten in a given span of time by all the members disturbing the rhythm of their family life. Late night movies disturbed their sleeping pattern and it was the families of the lower class which particularly felt its adverse effect, because they did not have weekend and had to work six or seven days a week.

To what extent, exposure to television commercials has

prompted the families to buy the products shown on television? An attempt was made to find out items which the families bought after being exposed to them on the television as well as to identify the members in the family on whose insistence those items were bought.

Instead of identifying the brands of particular items, we have divided the items bought under certain broad headings. At the outset it may be mentioned here that items bought by respondents after being exposed to television commercials do not mean that respondents were not using these items e.g., detergents and eatables. The responses have been tabulated keeping in view the new items and new brand names which they have bought after seeing them displayed on television.

Under the item eatables, families belonging to all the classes have been influenced and have bought items. However, it was noted that the items which were relatively costly were bought by the upper classes and items which were cheaper were acquired by families of the lower classes. Similar was the case with regard to soaps and detergents. A number of advertisements appear on television depicting the qualities of different detergents and soaps. It was noted that 'NIRMA' detergent was found to be more popular among the lower class whereas among the middle and upper classes costly detergents and soaps like Surf, Eazee, Crowning Glory, Dettol etc. were bought. The cosmetics shown on the television which were relatively costly had the clientage of the middle and upper classes. Similar was the case with regard to items like construction materials, clothes, shoes, machinery etc. as well as different investment schemes for providing social security and multiplication of money saved. Machinery like fridge, motor cycles, washing machines, etc. attracted the members of the middle and upper classes. It becomes quite obvious from the list of the items bought, that the items displayed on television are directed to attract the attention of the middle and upper classes and very few items are displayed which are cheaper and families of the lower classes could afford to buy those brand names.

In short, television commercials are also class oriented, i.e., the sponsors take into account the class background and the capabilities of the people to buy those items and accordingly they come up with certain commercials. Further, those manufacturers who produce cheaper items and have less capital cannot compete with the big business houses and hence do not display their items on television. Because they have certain clientage of the lower classes who buy their items even if they are attracted to other brand names. The buying habits of family are also governed by familial economic position. Irrespective of temptation they receive after being exposed to television commercials the viewers buy the advertised items if they have the resources.

The respondents were further asked to identify the members of the family on whose insistence they have bought the products shown on television. The tabulation of data revealed that the items of eatables attracted the attention of the younger generation and the children insisted their parents to buy those brands of eatables. We did not find any marked difference in the families of all the social classes represented in the study. With regard to the decisions to buy soaps, detergents, durables, utensils, cookers, cosmetics etc., it was the decision of the women of family because these items concerned them and they were the persons who were going to use these items. So far as other items which were costly e.g., buying motor cycles, fridge, washing machines or other durables, it was noted that the male heads in the families played an important role in selecting a particular brand, with the exception of buying of motor cycles which was on the insistence of grown up children in the families of the upper and middle classes. Investment in life insurance, medicare and other schemes under which one could earn higher interest came under the domain of the male heads of the families of the upper and middle classes. The members of the lower class also indicated the same patterns, though due to economic strains very few families had gone for such investments. Nevertheless, family power dynamics became quite obvious i.e., male head took the decision for investment on these items.

The respondents also opined that display of different items during the commercials created a need among them even when they did not require the items in the family. Buying the advertised new things and labels had put a strain on the tight family budget. It was more true in case of the families of the lower and middle classes. Further, inability on part of the parents to buy things as demanded by the children who had seen those items on television created unnecessary frustration and tensions. A few members also complained that they were misled by the advertisement. They bought certain things and brands after being exposed on television but did not find the quality of the brands as advertised on television. In short, commercials have created a felt need among the viewers to buy certain items and brands but have also created frustration among those who could not buy and such exposure has disturbed the family budget.

It is generally contended that programmes shown on television increase the extent and intensity of interaction between the family members because television viewing is a family activity and members of family sit together to watch the programmes. Further, programme contents provide topics and themes for lively family discussion and exchanges (Yadava and Reddy, 1988).

The respondents were asked, 'whether they discussed among the family members the programmes shown on television'? It is interesting to note that a majority of the families of the middle class (approximately 62 per cent) admitted that television programmes provided them subject matter and themes to discuss among themselves, particularly the theme, direction, acting as well as the way in which the theme depicted was likely to effect Indian Society. A majority of the families in the lower and upper classes denied that television provided lively themes for them to discuss.

Television viewing being a family activity provides an opportunity to the members of the family to sit together and watch the programme. This physical proximity before the television, no doubt, provides them an opportunity to converse with each other as well as discuss the themes shown in television programmes. There is, however, another side of picture--physical proximity with the introduction of television at home may increase but social togetherness may decrease. There is no communication among members hence television acts as anti-social. To what extent such negative effect of the television was perceived by our respondents?

TABLE 2.5: **The reactions of the members when someone converses when a popular programme was being shown**

| | Classes | | | |
|---|---|---|---|---|
| Reaction | Upper | Middle | Lower | Total |
| Shut him | 17 (27.42) | 62 (44.93) | 38 (38.00) | 117 (39.00) |
| Indifferent | 15 (24.19) | 16 (11.59) | 12 (12.00) | 43 (14.33) |
| Not applicable | 30 (48.39) | 60 (43.48) | 50 (50.00) | 140 (46.67) |
| Total | 62 (100.00) | 138 (100.00) | 100 (100.00) | 300 (100.00) |

Data on the reactions of the respondents revealed that in 140 families out of 300, conversations did not take place when some popular programmes were shown on television. It clearly indicates that in 47 per cent families under study there was no communication between the family members even though in the physical proximity to each other and were watching the same programme at the same time. The data further reveals that in those families when someone started talking, there was a sharp reaction from other members to such conversation. In case of families of the middle class the reaction was very sharp to stop the interrupting members, 45 per cent of the respondents indicated that if such a situation happened then the male head of the family normally asked the interrupting member to stop interruption followed by 38 per cent of the lower class families and 27 per cent of the upper class families. The reactions of the members to such conversation clearly indicated that physical proximity per se did not facilitate greater communication between the members of the family.

The foregoing discussion on the effects of television viewing helps us to conclude that television content has both positive and negative impact on family life. On the positive side, introduction of television in the family has disciplined the life of the members and has made them time conscious. Television is the cheapest source of entertainment and hence helps the family to save some money which normally they would spend on entertainment outside. Television has created an information revolution. Its informative and educative programmes open up the horizon of the people and make them aware about the happenings in the world and this is more true in case of illiterate and less educated population. Television programmes bring the family members together in the evenings and provide topics for discussion facilitating greater interaction among the members. Further exposure to different items and brands during the commercials make people aware about the competitive qualities of different brands, facilitating a greater selection.

Exposure to television commercials in the families of the lower and lower middle classes, on the other hand, has created problems of adjustment in the family budget. Exposure to new items and brands has, no doubt, created a felt need in the lower segments of society and their failure to buy those things has resulted into greater frustration. Further, physical proximity did not create greater cohesivenss, in spite of sitting together there was lack of communication between the members of the family. Additionally, introduction of television has adversely affected their routine life, disturbing their outings, and sleeping patterns.

The above discussion on consequences of television viewing on family supports the reciprocal influence hypothesis. On the one hand, introduction of television brings about changes in the routines of the families belonging to different classes. On the other hand, the social and cultural ethos of the families influence their television viewing. Further, familial power dynamics with regard to television viewing comes to the fore. The decision to buy certain items in the family were found to be related with stereotyped age and sex division. Children played an important role in persuading the parents to buy certain eatables displayed on television. Women bought items and brands related to their household work and men retained their right to buy durable machinery and expensive items. It was only in the upper class and few families of the middle class where grown up children also played an important role in deciding about the items to be bought. But in the families of the lower class the male dominance was quite evident. Family power dynamics have not been altered by the introduction of television rather, it becomes evident in their viewing behaviour pattern, selecting of programme, and family decision making process. In short, both television and family influence each other.

**Section B**

After having discussed the role of television viewing in the internal dynamics of family relations, we shall now take up the social interactions of the respondents outside their families. In this section, an attempt will be made to find out the extent to which introduction of television has promoted or hindered social interactions. We would also highlight the impact of television viewing on the activities of the members outside the family. Whether television programmes have put a wrench on their outside activities or have brought about modifications in such activities.

The respondents were asked, whether they visited their neighbours to watch some interesting television programmes when they were not having televsion sets of their own or when it went out of order.

A few respondents of the upper class (3.23 per cent) and 27.54 per cent of the middle class admitted that they had gone to their neighbours or other known persons to watch some interesting television programmes. A majority of them did not visit their neighbours for the sake of watching some television programmes. They opined that by doing so they would have down graded their own position. Further, they were not interested to encroach upon the privacy of their neighbours. On the other hand, 42 per cent respondents of the lower class admitted that they and their children were regularly going to the neighbours to watch some serials or other interesting television programmes.

The respondents were further asked, whether their neighbours and other known persons had come to their houses to watch television programmes since they themselves had bought television sets. It was again noted that a good number of respondents of the lower class and a few from the middle class confirmed that their neighbours and their children often visited their houses to watch some television programmes. In short, it can be concluded that television facilitated greater interaction among the neighbours of the lower class as compared with the upper classes.

In which way television hinders or promotes social interaction outside the family? The answer to this question was found out from the respondents by posing a question to them, what was their reaction, if someone visited them during an interesting television programme?

TABLE 2.6: **Reactions of the respondents when interrupted during an interesting television programme**

| Reactions | Classes | | | Total |
|---|---|---|---|---|
| | Upper | Middle | Lower | |
| Did not mind | 27 (43.55) | 38 (27.54) | 21 (21.00) | 86 (28.67) |
| Stopped television to attend to them | 12 (19.35) | 25 (18.11) | 2 (2.00) | 39 ( 13.00) |
| They also watched | 13 (20.97) | 36 (26.09) | 65 (65.00) | 114 (38.00) |
| Felt irritated | 10 (16.13) | 39 (28.26) | 12 (12.00) | 61 (20.33) |
| Total | 62 (100.00) | 138 (100.00) | 100 (100.00) | 300 (100.00) |

A majority of the respondents of the upper class 62.9 per cent did not negatively react to such interruptions. They did not mind their visits and switched off the television set to attend the visitors. In case of the middle class, approximately 45 per cent of the respondents did not feel bad, when interrupted during an interesting television programme. This percentage was reduced to only 23 per cent in case of the respondents of the lower class. With regard to the negative reaction of such interruptions, we noted that 28.26 per cent respondents of the middle class felt irritated, as compared with 16.30 per cent of the upper class respondents and only 12 per cent of the lower class. It is interesting to note that 65 per cent respondents of the lower class, 25.09 per cent of the middle class and 20.97 per cent of the upper class accommodated the visitors who also watched the programme being shown on television. Indirectly, these respondents admitted that there was no communication between the visitors and hosts when some interesting programmes were on and this was more true in case of the lower class as compared with the members of the upper class. A greater proportion of the respondents of the lower class who accommodated the visitors can be attributed to the common practice among the lower segments, who were either visiting their neighbours to watch television programmes or they were visited by their neighbours. Hence, visits during the television programmes was more common and accepted practice among them as compared with the respondents of the middle and upper classes. It can thus be concluded that television did not promote greater social interaction. Either the members felt irritated or somehow accommodated the visitors who were physically close to each other but there was no communication between them.

To what extent the introduction of television in their houses has brought about change in their outside activities? The activities include shopping, visiting friends, going to parties, and attending to other social calls.

TABLE 2.7: **Outside activities adversely affected after the introduction of television in their houses**

| | Classes | | | |
|---|---|---|---|---|
| Reaction | Upper | Middle | Lower | Total |
| Yes | 17<br>(27.42) | 75<br>(54.38) | 67<br>(67.00) | 159<br>(53.00) |
| No | 45<br>(72.58) | 63<br>(45.62) | 33<br>(33.00) | 141<br>(47.00) |
| Total | 62<br>(100.00) | 138<br>(100.00) | 100<br>(100.00) | 300<br>(100.00) |

A majority of the respondents of the upper class (72.58 per cent) contended that introduction of television in their homes has not affected their outside activities. Irrespective of the programmes they attended to social calls and participated in their usual activities outside their homes, because they felt that maintenance of social interaction outside the family was more important than watching television programme. The case of the respondents of the lower and middle classes was different. A majority of them (67 per cent of the lower class and 54.38 per cent of the middle class) admitted that television has forced them to change and readjust their outside activities in such a manner so that they did not come in the way of their watching some interesting television programmes. One-third respondents of the lower class, however, contended that because of the compulsion of work, despite their longing to watch television programme, they could not change their outside activities. The respondents of the middle class (45.62 per cent) felt that compulsion of social calls was greater than the attraction of television programme. Keeping in view the reactions of a majority of the respondents, it can be concluded that introduction of television has forced the members to modify their outside activities. The readjustment was more prominent among the respondents of the lower and middle classes. A majority of the respondents of the upper class, on the other hand, continued with their routine activities outside the family and were not motivated by television programmes to alter their routines.

The above analysis of the impact of television on social interaction outside the family helps us to conclude that television programmes do not promote social interaction outside the family. However, the members of different classes perceived the impact of television differently, implying thereby that their background affected their television viewing and social interaction outside their family, rather than television affecting their social interactions.

The last section of the chapter also supports the reciprocal influence hypothesis. It can thus be concluded that introduction of television in the family has brought about some changes in the internal dynamics of the family, as well as in their social interaction outside the family. On the other hand, class background of the family colours, controls and regulates their television viewing behaviour pattern.

# 3
# Television and Children

Children in the family are likely to be the most vulnerable population to be influenced by the contents of television transmission. Television acts as a source of information, education, entertainment and consumerism and it is through these functions that it is likely to influence the viewer. During the formative years of life, there is a curiosity among the children to know and learn new things from different sources and television contents play a significant role to meet their curiosity.

Television is treated as a medium through which people learn many things. Television when used for educational purposes has proved to be an excellent aid for learnig not only at classrooms but also at home (Comstock, et. al., 1978). Communication Research has yielded rich data pertaining to learning behaviour pattern of the children exposed to television programme. Bandura (1973, 1977, 1978) is of the view that social learning theory has been most interested in developing a model of the processes by which television contents influence child behaviour. In which way television content acts as a medium of socialization? Dorr (1986) is very explicit and contends that television plays four roles in children's lives--one is that of time consuming activity--a relaxing reward after work is done. Second is that of a social (non-social) event-- an opportunity to snuggle with parents or to escape from quarrelsome children. Third is that of informative processing task--a medium that requires looking and listening simultaneously and remembering a chain of events. Fourth and final role is that of an information -- providing experience-- a source of knowledge, what to buy, how to play, fight and love. While dealing the viewing patterns, Dorr (1986) also maintained that they not only changed with age but also differed in different social classes. In short, television is treated as a powerful source of information to the children who learn a number of things from its different programmes.

Children, however, are not free to accept and practice new things which come in their way. Being dependent upon the parents, source of the knowledge given on television as well as the contents of such knowledge are censored and controlled by parents. This is more true in case of children in the Indian families because of their dependency for a longer period. It is the parents who decide their style of life, friendship circle and the schools they attend. Similarly, parents are likely to control and regulate their television viewing behaviour pattern. Research on family's experience with television focuses on rules for viewing, particularly the explicit rules that parents may have about content and quality of programmes that their children are allowed to watch. These studies however examine outcome rather than the process of rule making (Goodman, 1983). They may not have been sufficiently sensitive to the implicit rules that govern family process. To understand this, one would have to ask, how rules about television viewing are made in family, who formulates and who enforces these rules. Answers to these questions would not only help us to know television viewing behaviour pattern of children, but also the power dynamics of the family.

Researches on television and children have concluded that television contents have both positive and negative consequences for the children. On the one hand, television viewing helps in seeking knowledge regarding different things and on the other hand, it inhibits children's imaginative abilities (Atkin, 1978; Comstock et. al., 1978; Dorr, 1986; Singer, 1982).

To find out the impact of television viewing on children, the present chapter has been divided into 3 parts: (i) Television viewing behaviour pattern; (ii) motivation for television viewing; and (iii) impact of television viewing.

Under television viewing behaviour pattern, an attempt is made to find out the time children spend on television viewing. Whether television viewing brings about change in the routine, if yes, what type of readjustment they make? Further, an attempt is made to find out the extent to which children are free to watch the programmes of their liking and the ways in which parents control and regulate their television viewing.

Keeping in view the main functions of television in India, the motivation for children to watch television programmes will be identified. Further, the role of parents in motivating the children to watch television programmes or to inhibit their television viewing of certain programmes will also be analysed.

In the last section of this chapter both positive and negative impacts of television viewing on children keeping in view their social class background will be analysed. In short, this chapter addresses to three main questions: what time the children spend on television watching, why they watch television programmes and with what effects. It may be added here that responses to these questions were not secured from the children themselves but from their mothers who were the respondents for the present study. Further, the number of children varied from family to family hence instead of taking into account the number of children we have tabulated data according to number of households under study.

**Children Television Viewing Behaviour Pattern**

Researches on the patterns of television viewing by children indicate that children in the families of the lower social class watch television for longer duration than those higher in status (Dorr, 1986). The amount of time spent on television viewing has been analysed keeping in view the number of hours on an average children spend on television viewing.

The children of the upper social class watch television for lesser duration as compared with children of the middle and lower classes. In case of the children of the upper class 72.58 per cent watched television on an average for 2 hours or less per day. This percentage came down to 39.86 per cent in case of children of the middle class and further decreased to 19 per cent for the lower class. Conversely, 81 per cent children belonging to the lower class watched television on an average for more than 2 hours daily and 60.14 per cent children of the middle class and only 27.42 per cent of the upper class watched television for such longer duration. The tabulation helps us to conclude that there is inverse relation between social class of the children and amount of time spent on television watching i.e., the higher the class, the lower the amount of time spent on television watching and conversely the lower the class, the greater the time spent on television watching. The results of the study support the contention of Dorr (1986).

The parents were further asked, whether their children of school going age group have rescheduled their routine to watch Doordarshan programmes.

**TABLE 3.1 : Distribution of children who made adjustment of their routine to watch Doordarshan by class**

| | Classes | | | |
|---|---|---|---|---|
| Adjustment made | Upper | Middle | Lower | Total |
| Yes | 27 (43.55) | 68 (49.28) | 33 (33.00) | 128 (42.67) |
| No | 25 (40.32) | 45 (32.60) | 40 (40.00) | 110 (36.67) |
| N. A. | 10 (16.13) | 25 (18.12) | 27 (27.00) | 62 (20.66) |
| Total | 62 (100.00) | 138 (100.00) | 100 (100.00) | 300 (100.00) |

Approximately 44 per cent respondents of the upper class contended that their children had readjusted their routine with regard to doing home work and play activities so that they could watch television programmes of their liking. This percentage was relatively higher (49.28 per cent) in the case of children of the middle class. Only one-third children of the lower class have rescheduled their routine activities. The respondents who gave negative response to the question, gave different reasons for the non-disturbance of the routine of their children. The respondents of the upper class observed that the routine for doing their home work and play activity were not disturbed either because they did not collide with Doordarshan programmes or the children were not interested in watching them. So far as the parents of the children of the middle class are concerned, they felt that children were more interested to pursue their studies rather than watching Doordarshan programme. Further, their home work and play activities were over by the time the serials and other interesting programmes were shown on Doordarshan. The respondents of the lower class, on the other hand, confessed that their children were addicted to television and they did their home work while watching television programmes. They attributed this to lack of space in their houses. Further, their children hardly spent any time on play activities. Hence the question of rescheduling did not arise.

With regard to existence of family rules pertaining to children television viewing, the respondents were asked, how have they regulated television viewing behaviour pattern of their children.

TABLE 3.2 : **Television watching rules for the children by class**

| Rules | Classes | | | Total * |
|---|---|---|---|---|
| | Upper | Middle | Lower | |
| Not allowed to switch on the television set | 11 | 32 | 40 | 83 |
| Not allowed to watch all the programmes | 32 | 69 | 17 | 118 |
| Can't watch unless complete their home work and studies and other activities | 25 | 62 | 30 | 117 |
| Allowed to watch for a fixed period of time | 31 | 73 | 12 | 116 |
| Allowed to watch children programmes | 12 | 23 | 18 | 53 |
| Allowed to watch entertainment programmes (Chitrahaars and movies) | 22 | 45 | 60 | 127 |

*Multiple choices were allowed.

The respondents of the upper and middle classes were quite explicit in maintaining that their children were not allowed to watch all the programmes shown on television.

On the other hand, they were allowed to watch for a fixed period of time indicating that children's television viewing was controlled and regulated by parents and children were not free to watch the programme as and when they liked to. Such a situation clearly indicates the control of the parents over their children's television viewing behaviour pattern. However, parental control decreased with the increase in the age group of their children. The grown up children of the upper and middle classes who had VCP/VCR or cable networks watched television according to their liking and free time at their disposal. In short, control over television watching was exercised by the parents on small children in the family. The case of the respondents of the lower class was relatively different. No doubt, 40 per cent of the respondents maintained that their children were not allowed to handle the television sets. Yet, very few respondents were able to impose certain rules with regard to their children's television viewing. The lack of control is attributed to the fact that most of them lived in one room house, hence could not regulate television viewing by their children. The analysis helps us to conclude that a majority of the parents in the upper and middle classes have framed television watching rules for the children i.e., when to watch television and for what duration of time and what type of programmes they watch. The parents of the lower class due to shortage of space could not effectively implement these rules.

To find out the extent of control parents have over their children's television viewing behaviour pattern, the respondents were specifically asked, 'whether the children watched late night movies?' It may be added that Delhi Doordarshan has recently started screening late night movies which are meant for adults only.

As compared with 48 per cent children of the lower class, 27.42 per cent of the upper class and 20.29 per cent of the middle class children watched late night movies. This clearly indicates that parents of the lower class did not have control over their children for watching late night movies. The respondents of the lower class could not check their children for watching late night movies because of the shortage of space and placement of television set in their houses. A few respondents, however, informed that because of space problem they also did not watch such movies. In case of the upper and middle classes a majority of the parents still exerted control over their children so far as their television watching programmes meant for adults were concerned.

Confining our discussion to only 93 cases where children watched late night movies, the respondents were asked, whether their children watched such programmes with or without their permission.

The tabulation of the data reveals that in the lower class more than 54 per cent children watched late night movies without the permission of their parents. As compared with this 23.53 per cent respondents of the upper class and only 14.29 per cent of the middle class admitted their lack of control over their children, so far their late night movie watching behaviour was concerned. This admission on part of the parents clearly indicates that television is becoming a powerful stimulator and has even eroded the authority of the parents, even though limited to a small number of cases. It was in the case of the middle class only where a higher percentage of parents had control over their children television viewing behaviour pattern. The respondents of the lower class admitted that because of lack of space they could not regulate their children's watching late night movies.

The discussion on time spent on television watching by the children in the family helps us to conclude that not only the time spent by children on television watching was class based but their television watching was regulated and controlled by their parents which was more true in case of parents of the upper and middle classes.

**Motivation for Television Viewing**

After having analysed television watching behaviour pattern of the children as perceived by their parents, we shall now take up different programmes which children in families normally watch and their motivations. As discussed earlier different programmes shown on Doordarshan were grouped under the categories of education, information and entertainment and combinations thereof. The parents were asked which programmes their children normally watched.

TABLE 3.3: **Programmes normally watched by children**

| | Classes | | | |
|---|---|---|---|---|
| Programmes | Upper | Middle | Lower | Total* |
| Entertainment | 32 | 67 | 100 | 199 |
| Educational | 38 | 69 | 33 | 140 |
| Informational | 37 | 69 | 23 | 129 |

*Multiple choices were allowed.

Looking at the programmes watched by the children of different class background it becomes clear that children of the lower class are more interested in programmes of entertainment. Taking into account the educative and informative programmes of television, children of the upper and middle classes have greater representation and very few children of lower class watched such programmes. In the case of children of the upper and middle classes there was almost equal distribution of children who watched these programmes. Whereas in the case of children of the lower class all the children watched programmes of entertainment and only one-third watched educative programmes and approximately one-fourth watched informative programmes. It can thus be concluded that children of the lower class watch television for entertainment whereas children of the upper and middle classes treat television content as a source of education and information in addition to entertainment. Those parents who had VCR/VCP and access to cable networks also contended that their children watched programmes of their liking, e.g., Hindi and English movies, Newstrack, English songs and other programmes of their liking because they did not find Doordarshan programmes entertaining.

What are the motivations for the children to watch different Doordarshan programmes? Most of the parents of the lower class contend that television viewing has become a habit with their children and they watch television to pass time. Further, television is the cheapest source of entertainment to them and they are allowed to watch television, so that they remain at home and do not loiter outside. Their television watching also helps them to be free from fights with their peers when they go out. As compared with this most of the parents of the upper and middle classes maintained that their children watched Doordarshan for relaxation as well as for getting information and learning new things. They encouraged their children to watch sports, quiz, focus, current affairs etc. which would help them to learn new things and be acquainted with latest developments. Parents of the upper and middle classes who had connections for cable networks contended that their children were being influenced by foreign transmission as these programmes provided a greater variety and entertainment to them. Their children preferred cable transmission over Doordarshan programmes because they felt that the quality of Doordarshan programmes was quite low. Cable transmission according to these parents has become a source of relaxation, enjoyment as well as more informative.

To what extent the contention of the parents of the upper and middle classes is correct? For this purpose we specifically asked those parents who had children in age group of 13-16 years, whether their children watched University Grants Commission programmes of Doordarshan which was specifically meant for students of eighth to tenth classes?

Out of 300 respondents only 131 respondents had children in age group of 13 to 16 years. A few respondents had only one child and others had 2/3 children in this age group. The tabulation clearly indicates that only a few children watched University Grants Commission (U.G.C.) programmes. Out of 131 respondents who had children in age group of 13 to 16 years, only 26 respondents admitted that their children watched the educative programmes sponsored by U.G.C. Out of 26 respondents who admitted that their children watched such programmes, 25 belonged to the upper and middle classes. Despite their lower number, the class background in watching educative programmes becomes quite obvious.

The respondents were further asked, what do their children learn from such programmes? The respondents maintained that the programmes were related to science subjects and were very educative and useful to their children. A majority of the respondents of the upper and middle classes whose children did not watch U.G.C. programmes contended that the timings at which these programmes were shown, were not suitable to their children. During the noon transmission they were at the school and in the afternoon transmission they were busy with home work or play activities, hence could not watch them. The mothers of the children of the lower class informed us that the contents of such programmes were beyond the comprehension of their children. The contents were technical and were delivered in English or Sanskritized Hindi, hence, their children did not show any interest in the programmes even when they were free to watch them.

The description on the type of programmes watched by children makes it clear that not only the children belonging to different classes watch different programmes but their motivations for watching them also differ according to their class background.

Television in India being commercial has another important function to perform i.e. to push up the sale of certain consumer items. The advertisers show child artists in the advertisements to attract the child population for buying their products. How far the children of the respondents under study have been influenced by these advertisements? We asked the respondents, whether they switched on the television on the insistence of the children, so that they could also watch the commercials?

More than three-fourths of the respondents of the lower class confessed that on the insistence of their children, they switched on the television at the announced time for a particular programme even though they were aware, that the actual programme would come after 10 to 15 minutes. They switch on the television so that they and their children could watch commercials also. As compared with this only 50 per cent of the respondents of the middle class and only one-third of the upper class admitted that they switched on the television at the announced time so that the children could watch commercials. It becomes quite clear that the child population of the lower and middle classes is more vulnerable to the advertisements shown on Doordarshan. The situation is relatively different for those who watch cable transmission because commercials are shown repeatedly in-between the programmes.

Have the parents bought certain commodities on the insistence of their children? A good proportion of the respondents belonging to the lower and middle classes admitted that they had bought a number of items, particularly eatables on the insistence of their children who were exposed to these items on Doordarshan. The respondents of the upper class also admitted that their children bought certain items on their own after being influenced by commercials on Doordarshan. A few respondents of the upper classes further informed us that their children were developing craze for foreign stuff after being exposed to the commercials on cable networks. However middle class respondents did not endorse it. Taking into account the replies of our respondents it is clear that children are becoming new decision makers in family and after being exposed to different items they force their parents to buy certain items, particularly the eatables. It does not, however, mean that family decision making authority of the parents has been eroded. It, however, implies that children are now becoming more aware about different things and they insist that their parents buy those things. In short, children are being influenced by different commercials and it is perhaps for this reason that the advertisers are not putting up more and more child artists in their commercials.

**Impact of Television Viewing**

The respondents are likely to perceive both positive and negative consequences of television watching on their children. Let us first of all take up the positive impact of television contents as perceived by the respondents.

Television has ushered in information revolution. Children are now better equipped with knowledge regarding different places in India and other nations. They have come to know about different styles of life and have learned to develop greater tolerance towards people of other faiths. A majority of the respondents of the upper and middle classes felt that their children learnt many new things from television contents and became more aware about realities of life. Things which they could not understand and remember after reading books could now be easily comprehended through television. Programmes like 'Discovery of India' helped their children to know more about India. The epic stories of `Ramayana' and `Mahabharatha' helped them to know more about our cultural ethos. Similarly, serial depicting rural life in India facilitated their children to know the pitiable conditions of rural poor without having been to a village. They however felt that television medium acts as a one way communication. When the children had certain doubts and questions to ask, there was no one to give the appropriate answers. The respondents who had connection for cable transmission further opined that their children had become more knowledgeable with the cultural ethos of other countries.

The respondents of the lower class opined that their children used to loiter around and indulged into different mischiefs and quarrels. They were fed up with the complaints against their children. The respondents felt that with the introduction of television sets in their homes, their children had started spending more time inside the house. Thus, their children were saved from bad company. These respondents felt happy that with television at home, their children were not interested to see movies at the cinema halls, thus saved them from such expenditure. A few respondents who had adolescent children opined that television at home has reduced truancy of their children, who used to abstain from the school/college to see morning film shows at cinema halls. The respondents perceived television as a cheapest mode of entertainment for the whole family. The respondents also treated television as a medium through which they and their children learned many new things and it was an important source of information and learning.

TABLE 3.4 : **Distribution of respondents class-wise who perceived positive consequences of television watching on their children**

| | Classes | | | |
|---|---|---|---|---|
| Effects | Upper | Middle | Lower | Total |
| Increase their knowledge | 21 (33.88) | 41 (29.71) | 13 (13.00) | 75 (25.00) |
| Greater awareness about recent events | 18 (29.03) | 30 (21.74) | 5 (5.00) | 53 (17.66) |
| Sit at home | 7 (11.29) | 26 (18.84) | 21 (21.00) | 54 (18.00) |
| Cheap entertainment | 8 (12.90) | 20 (14.49) | 35 (35.00) | 63 (21.00) |
| No positive impact | 8 (12.90) | 21 (15.22) | 26 (26.00) | 55 (18.34) |
| Total | 62 (100.00) | 138 (100.00) | 100 (100.00) | 300 (100.00) |

Out of 128 respondents who perceived that television watching increased the knowledge of the children as well as made them more aware about recent events, a majority of them belonged to the upper and middle classes. On the other hand, out of the 117 respondents who perceived that with the introduction of television at home, their children now spent more time at home and television was also a source of entertainment to children at low cost, 56 respondents were from the lower class and only 15 respondents of the upper class perceived such a positive impact of television on their children. In addition to these, there were 55 respondents mostly from the lower and middle classes who did not perceive any positive impact of television viewing on their children. Taking into account the perceived positive consequences of television viewing on children, it becomes clear that respondents having different social background perceived the positive impact of television viewing on their children differently. In short, class of the parents played an important role in their perception of the positive impact of television watching. It does not, however, mean that these respondents have not perceived negative consequences of television watching. Respondents who perceived positive impact of television viewing also identified a number of negative consequences of television watching on their children.

The respondents perceived that television watching by their children had adversely effected their studies. They hurriedly completed their home work and even did it while watching television programmes. They lacked concentration and refrained from reading newspaper, magazines etc. The exposure to commercials have made their children more demanding type. The children were becoming more obstinate and were annoyed in case the parents failed to meet their demands. The respondents felt that their children did not listen to them, they were more influenced by television programmes and sometimes questioned parental authority.

The children have started treating the hero in the programmes as their referent or 'model'. A few respondents were quite explicit, they revealed that their children after watching cable transmission had started copying the western way of life particularly with regard to dress and had developed taste for western music and dance. The children were inculcating western mode of life and did not indicate any appreciation for Indian cultural ethos.

The demands for new things have put a constraint on the family budget which was felt more by the respondents of the lower and middle classes. The respondents opined that television had introduced their children to an adult world resulting into disappearance of their childhood. The children after being exposed to television matured earlier than their age, which would have bad consequences for their future life. Such a negative effect was perceived more by those parents who had access to cable networks. The respondents further opined that with the introduction of television at their homes, their children had stopped a number of outdoor activities like play, interaction with their peers and felt that television watching was a mere waste of time for them. They also felt that their children have developed passivity. A few respondents of the lower class felt that television watching had also adversely affected their eyesight. In short, the respondents admitted that television has assumed the status of an agent of socialization in the family for their children and they learnt many things, though most of them were bad.

There were only 27 respondents, mostly from the upper and middle classes who did not perceive any negative impact of television. Out of those who perceived that television watching adversely affected the studies of their children and made them obstinate, a majority of them were from the lower and middle classes. In case of those respondents who perceived that exposure to television content would make the children mature earlier than their age, a majority of them had the middle class background. Similarly, among those

TABLE 3.5: Distribution of respondents class-wise who perceived negative consequences of television watching on their children

| Effect | Classes | | | Total |
|---|---|---|---|---|
| | Upper | Middle | Lower | |
| Lack initiative | 22 (35.48) | 11 (7.97) | 3 (3.00) | 36 (12.00) |
| Waste of time | 5 (8.06) | 25 (18.12) | 14 (14.00) | 44 (14.67) |
| Become demanding/ obstinate | 9 (14.52) | 31 (22.46) | 25 (25.00) | 65 (21.67) |
| Effect studies | 7 (11.29) | 32 (23.19) | 30 (30.00) | 69 (23.00) |
| Mature early | 9 (14.52) | 21 (15.22) | 16 (16.00) | 46 (15.33) |
| Eyesight | | 3 (2.17) | 10 (10.00) | 13 (4.33) |
| No negative effect | 10 (16.13) | 15 (10.87) | 2 (2.00) | 27 (9.00) |
| Total | 62 (100.00) | 138 (100.00) | 100 (100.00) | 300 (100.00) |

who felt that television watching resulted into wastage of time of their children, a majority came from the middle class followed by the respondents of the lower and upper classes. Among those who perceived that regular television watching adversely affected the eyesight of their children, a majority came from the lower class and not a single respondent from the upper class felt that television watching had adverse consequences on the eyesight of their children. With regard to 36 respondents who opined that television watching adversely affected the imaginative and creative abilities, a majority were from the upper and middle classes and very few from the lower class perceived this negative effect of television. The respondents felt that 'Hum Aur Aap' ( we and you) Doordarshan programme (where letters from the viewers were taken up) failed to give right and appropriate answers to their children s questions pertaining to television contents. Hence indifference on the part of programme producers as well as Doordarshan authorities dampened their interest and initiative capabilities. The analysis helps us to conclude that perception of negative consequences of television watching on children was based on the class background of the respondents.

The correlation between the amount of time spent on television viewing and effect of television watching were not worked out because, firstly, we were not able to isolate the effect of television watching from other influences on the children. Secondly, the children of the upper and middle classes who watched Doordarshan programmes for lesser duration spent more time on VCR/VCP and watching cable networks. Hence, the total amount of time spent on programmes watching through VCR/VCP/CTV compensated the less time spent on Doordarshan programme watching. In short, children of all classes spent almost same time.

Keeping in view the perception of the respondents regarding positive and negative consequences of television watching on their children, it becomes clear that television has assumed an important position in the family. It acts as an agent of socialization for children, whether the children learn new things, enhance their knowledge or inhibit their imaginative or creative abilities or waste their time at the cost of their studies. The respondents have implicitly admitted that with the introduction of television their authority is being eroded and children are under the spell of television. It does not, however, mean that television has replaced the parents as agent of socialization. It may, however, be added that the degree of attention which children give to television content is dependent upon the parents who decide about the priorities for their children.

The very fact that parents belonging to different strata perceived both positive and negative consequences of television watching on their children differently, indicated that family background played an important role in determining television watching behaviour pattern, motivation for television viewing and the impact of television content on the children. In short, this chapter on television and children also supported the reciprocal influence hypothesis i.e., television effects children in the family and family influences television viewing behaviour pattern of the children.

# 4

# Programmes and Their Evaluation

The communication researcher James Lull (cited by Dorr, 1986) has proposed a typology for the social uses of television: structural and functional. When it is used in structural ways, television provides reassuring background noise and companionship (Environmental use) and a means for marking time and organising activity (Regulative use). When it is used in relational ways television provides subject matter for conversation (Communication facilitation), opportunities for physical and emotional contact (Affiliation/avoidance), potentially useful examples of interpersonal interactions (Social learning) and opportunities to enact roles and power relationships (Competence/dominance). Whether or not this typology is entirely correct it nicely illustrates the range of social uses that the television viewing event permits.

Television in India, was introduced by the Government with the specific purpose of information dissemination, educating the people about different problems the country was facing and for the entertainment of the viewers. Nevertheless, television in India is predominantly for entertainment (Tribune, Sept. 14, 1989). Since its introduction it has remained under the control of the Government. Its programme contents are censored and only those contents which get Government approval are shown.

No doubt the main attraction of television remains in its entertainment programmes, the means by which it attracts the viewers, it also inevitably informs them. Through its varied programmes the audience is exposed to the unknown as well as the confirmation of the known. It is perhaps in this context that Comstock opines that television serves, "curiosity, the will to experience and understand, the longing to enter the imaginery, the impulse to engage in imagination and the mind in something that is real enough, yet distant enough from everyday life" (Comstock, 1980, p. 126). Despite greater emphasis on entertainment to attract audience the basic function of television in India remains to be informative. For the purpose of understanding the role of television content in everyday life of the viewers, it is important to divide the process of knowledge transmission into information dissemination, information interpretation and evaluation of the information given on television. It may, however, be added that information dissemination, interpretive and evaluative activities all occur at one time or another in the course of making sense of television content.

Doordarshan through its varied programmes, news, serials, discussion on current topics, world affairs etc. makes people aware about what is happening in the country and outside, as well as makes them conscious about different social issues and problems our country is facing. The objective of information dissemination is well served by television through its visual drama of the events it depicts on the small screen. Information dissemination activities lead to the extraction of concrete and literal meaning for television content. They involve choosing among and acting upon the auditory and visual stimuli provided by television without going beyond them. Interpretive activities go beyond these facts to supply content that is suggested but not actually depicted, to understand feelings and motives and to string together pieces of content to form a larger whole. Interpretive activities in a sense create meanings. Evaluative activities add reactions to denotative and connotative, explicit and implicit meaning. They involve creating pro or con, liking or disliking relationship with the content (Dorr, 1986). He further opines: "Information is believed to influence attitudes and behaviors and attitudes are believed to influence behaviors. Informational effects are easiest to obtain, attitudinal effects are harder and behavioral effects are hardest" (Dorr, 1986, p. 67).

Keeping in view the above observations, the present chapter has been divided into two parts: information dissemination and evaluation. Under information dissemination, an attempt will be made to find out from the respondents the issues on which they were made more aware by their exposure to Doordarshan contents. They were also asked to identify the programmes which made them aware about the issues. An attempt was also made to find out, as to how people with different social class background and value system perceived these programmes and what meaning they attached. After having been made aware about the problems, were they able to bring about change in their opinion and attitudes regarding these issues and in which way they brought about some changes in their behaviour pattern and social interactions.

In the last section of this chapter an attempt was made to find out the reactions of the respondents to Doordarshan programmes. Did they perceive Doordarshan contents desirable or undesirable; censored and twisted or depicted reality. Their opinions were also sought regarding Government control over television and were they in favour of granting autonomy to television and having private channels so that they could have free flow of information as well as wider coverage to the information. Additionally, the respondents who had access to cable network were asked to give their opinion regarding cable network transmission vis-a-vis Doordarshan programmes.

## Section A

### Information Dissemination and Its Interpretation

The respondents were asked to identify the issues on which they became more aware after viewing different Doordarshan programmes. They were further asked to identify the specific programme which highlighted those issues, and what meaning they attached to those television contents. In other words, how did they make use of the information received. The respondents, who did not perceive television information as issue oriented, were asked to point out the pitfalls of such programmes. It was expected that the respondents belonging to the lower strata would depend upon Doordarshan transmission more for attaining such information as compared with respondents of the upper and middle classes. As members of the lower class were either illiterate or less educated they could not make use of other channels of mass communication like newspapers, magazines etc. to get additional and objective information.

### Health Awareness

India remains basically a rural society as more than two-thirds of its population are residing in rural areas, which lack basic amenities of life. Further, a majority of the rural people and particularly the women folk are illiterate. Hence are unaware about the precautions to be taken against different diseases. Their ignorance and beliefs in traditions and lack of medical facilities were basically responsible for high fertility and mortality. Television in India was used to make people aware about different health hazards and the precautions to

TABLE 4.1 : Perception of the respondents classwise that Doordarshan contents were propagating health awareness

| Perception | Classes | | | |
|---|---|---|---|---|
| | Upper | Middle | Lower | Total |
| Yes | 20<br>(32.26) | 72<br>(52.17) | 62<br>(62.00) | 154<br>(51.34) |
| No | 20<br>(32.26) | 38<br>(27.54) | 30<br>(30.00) | 88<br>(29.33) |
| No response | 22<br>(35.48) | 28<br>(20.29) | 8<br>(8.00) | 58<br>(19.33) |
| Total | 62<br>(100.00) | 138<br>(100.00) | 100<br>(100.00) | 300<br>(100.00) |

be taken against different diseases. Doordarshan clipping on 'Teen Tike' (Three vaccinations) has been an integral part of daily television transmission. Similarly, different documentaries and health oriented programmes are being shown to make people aware about health and its related problems.

The respondents who became more aware about their health and related issues, identified the programmes like 'Jan Hai Jahan Hai' (health is wealth), 'Tuhadi Sehat' (your health), 'Stay-fit exercises', 'Yoga' and home made medicines to control different diseases. The respondents of the lower class (62 per cent) informed that they became aware about different diseases like Blindness, Diptheria, Whooping cough, Tetanus and Polio in children due to lack of balanced diet and timely vaccinations. They were made aware about the importance of green vegetables for the children and tried to cook such food for their young children. Similarly, the respondents with small children admitted that they had become very particular about timely vaccination. Similarly, they became very cautious about drinking water, as they had become aware that water was the main carrier of different diseases.Further, keeping in view their resources they were trying to keep cleanliness in their surroundings. In case of the respondents of the upper class, a majority of them contended that they were already aware about the precautions to be taken to maintain good health. Approximately 32 per cent admitted that they learnt new things from Doordarshan health oriented programmes. A few respondents admitted that they followed the instructions given on television under the programme of 'Stay fit exercises' and 'Yoga' and even tried to practise in front of their television sets when such programmes were on. They however complained that different exercises and postures were shown in quick succession, hence they could not keep pace with the programmes. More than 52 per cent respondents of the middle class have also benefited from different programmes pertaining to health. They identified Doordarshan programmes in which medical doctors gave advice regarding precautions to be taken for maintaining good health. They were also benefited from the programme of 'Stay fit exercises'. The respondents admitted that after watching such programmes they have become more cautious about balanced diet. In short, 154 respondents (51.34 per cent) belonging to different classes admitted that they were made more aware about health and the precautions to be taken to maintain good health through their exposure to television content.

The respondents of the lower class (30 per cent) who did not perceive Doordarshan programmes being very helpful in creating health awareness, contended that programmes were highly elitist. They further opined that the programme contents should be such, that people with no knowledge of English could understand them. They further lamented that they could not follow the advice given by doctors on television, because of their inability to comprehend English words used in the programmes. Further, they felt that by simply making people aware about balanced diet would not help because of their inability to have balanced diet. The respondents of the upper and middle classes who felt that Doordarshan contents had failed to propagate health awareness, opined that such programmes did not touch the main issue of poverty and ignorance among the Indian masses.

**Population Problem**

With the help of medical facilities death rate has been brought down. However no appreciable decline in the fertility has taken place. Such a situation has resulted into increase in the population. Indian population which in 1951was 361 million increased to over 860 million in 1991 and is expected to cross one billion by 2001 A.D. To check the population growth the Government of India is propagating family planning measures through Doordarshan and other mass media. It is being advocated that different developmental activities which have been taken up by the government would not give the desired benefits to the people because of the rapid growth in the population. A small family norm with two children is being propagated so that the parents could look after their children properly. Different serials, documentaries and television clippings are being shown on

**TABLE 4.2 : Perception of the respondents class-wise that Doordarshan contents were making people aware about population problem**

| | Classes | | | |
|---|---|---|---|---|
| Making aware | Upper | Middle | Lower | Total |
| Yes | 15<br>(24.19) | 60<br>(43.48) | 61<br>(61.00) | 136<br>(45.34) |
| No | 22<br>(35.48) | 48<br>(34.78) | 30<br>(30.00) | 100<br>(33.00) |
| No response | 25<br>(40.33) | 30<br>(21.74) | 9<br>(9.00) | 64<br>(21.33) |
| Total | 62<br>(100.00) | 138<br>(100.00) | 100<br>(100.00) | 300<br>(100.00) |

Indian television to make the people aware about the growth of Indian population and its associated consequences. Let us find out the perception of our respondents to Doordarshan contents propagating family planning and in which way they have been motivated to control the population growth.

A majority of the respondents of the lower class (61.00 per cent) and 43.48 per cent of the middle class respondents admitted that they became more aware about the population problem of India after being exposed to television clips and different programmes. The respondents of the lower class were influenced by the programme highlighting spacing between the two children. A few respondents admitted that they had gone for sterilization and also started using condoms etc. to plan the size of their family. They however admitted that they could do so, only when their husbands agreed. A majority of the respondents of the upper and middle classes were already aware about the methods to be adopted to have small size of family as well as to have proper spacing between the two children. Nevertheless, 43.48 per cent respondents of the middle class and 24.19 per cent of the upper class admitted that they became more aware about population problem of India when it was shown on television the rapid rate of population growth (Increase of 48 children per minute), and how it would jeopardise all developmental activities undertaken after Independence.

Approximately one-third of the respondents felt that Doordarshan contents have failed to bring about any change in the attitudes of the people pertaining to the optimum size of the family because television documentaries, clippings and other programmes did not touch the main issue. The respondents of the upper and middle classes opined that unless preference for male child was not removed, people would continue to have more children in the hope of getting a male child. The respondents of the lower class, on the other hand, lamented that size of the family was not determined by them but by their husbands. They are completely under the control of their menfolk. This is further supported by the fact that those respondents who have gone for sterilization have done so with the consent of their husbands. In short, the respondents were of the opinion that unless values in favour of having a male child and discrimination against a female child were removed, television contents to control family would have no impact on the people.

**Age at Marriage**

Age at marriage has a direct bearing on population growth. The lower the age at marriage, the higher will be the fertility span of a woman. Such a contention is more true in Indian society, because age at marriage on an average has been 16 years for girls. Realising the importance of age at marriage the Government of India has legally advanced the age at marriage for women at 18 years and for men at 21 years. In spite of such legal provisions, the age at marriage has remained quite low, particularly in the rural areas. The impact of local traditions and belief in marrying the daughters at lower age were more powerful than the official dictates. To bring about change in the traditional attitudes, the Government of India through television clippings, documentaries and other serials is propagating for increase in the age at marriage. These documentaries highlight the ill effects of early marriage on the health of the mother as well as the

TABLE 4.3 : **Perception of the respondents class-wise that Doordarshan contents were making people aware about the desired age at marriage**

| | Classes | | | |
|---|---|---|---|---|
| Aware about right age | Upper | Middle | Lower | Total |
| Yes | 4 (6.45) | 25 (18.11) | 79 (79.00) | 108 (36.00) |
| No | 22 (35.49) | 62 (44.93) | 18 (18.00) | 102 (34.00) |
| No response | 36 (58.06) | 51 (36.96) | 3 (03.00) | 90 (30.00) |
| Total | 62 (100.00) | 138 (100.00) | 100 (100.00) | 300 (100.00) |

new born babies so that people are motivated to marry their children at higher age. Let us see in which way Doordarshan contents were able to disseminate the information pertaining to age at marriage and how such information was interpreted by the respondents.

Age at marriage was another issue which attracted the attention of a majority of the respondents (79 per cent) of the lower class. They admitted that they were marrying their children at younger age but now they have become aware that marriage at younger age has adverse effects on the health of their married daughters and also results into higher fertility and mortality. They were very much influenced by the television programme which depicted the suffering of a girl married at a lower age. They would like to marry their daughters only after the age of 18 years. The respondents of the upper and middle classes were already aware about the optimum age of marriage of their children and the television clips were actually directed towards the lower segment of society to make them aware about age at marriage and its consequences. Those who became more aware, identified television programmes, which depicted pitiable condition of the girls married at younger age. A few respondents of the upper and middle classes told us that they have even tried to persuade their servants and other members of the lower class not to marry their daughters at young age.

Approximately one-third of our respondents did not feel that by simply watching Doordarshan clippings and documentaries people would start marrying their children at an appropriate age. The respondents of the upper and middle classes felt that the hold of social customs and traditions was very strong in the Indian society. Unless these traditions change, television contents would not have the desired effect on the audience. They further opined that illiteracy and ignorance were the basic reasons for low age at marriage. Unless the government does something in this direction, television clippings and documentaries would not have the desired results. Eighteen per cent respondents of the lower class contended that the final authority in the family was with the menfolk, it is they who settle the marriage of their children and unless their opinions and attitudes change, age at marriage in their families would remain low.

**Dowry**

Marriage in India is a sacrament rather than a social contract. However, with the growing materialism the practice of dowry is fast changing the marriage institution into a commercial proposition. The evils of dowry have undermined the sanctity attached to this institution. Recently, the evil has assumed different dimension and a number of young married women are being harassed for not bringing sufficient dowry. The ill treatment and harassment have resulted into a number of dowry deaths and the conscience of the people has been shaken. The case of three sisters committing suicide at Kanpur because of the failure of the parents to arrange sufficient dowry for their marriage is a black spot on the Indian society. The Government of India through the medium of Doordarshan is making the public aware about the evils of dowry so that people refrain from such evil practices.

Doordarshan programmes depicting the evils of dowry attracted the attention of the middle and lower classes and they became more aware about its evils after watching a few serials. The fact that very few respondents belonging to the upper class were made aware about the evils of dowry indicated that either they were not having dowry practices or they were not facing the problems associated with dowry because they were resourceful enough to meet the demands of the bridegroom and his family. A few studies conducted in India have already highlighted that dowry is the problem of the lower and middle classes (Ahuja, 1987). It is perhaps for this reason that a majority of respondents of the lower and middle classes have become more aware about the evils of dowry after viewing Doordarshan programmes. A few respondents from the middle class informed that they had decided not to give or take dowry in the marriages of their children, whenever they took place. These respondents,

TABLE 4.4 : **Perception of the respondents class-wise that Doordarshan contents were making people aware about the evils of dowry**

| | Classes | | | |
|---|---|---|---|---|
| Evils of dowry | Upper | Middle | Lower | Total |
| Yes | 8<br>(12.90) | 71<br>(51.45) | 69<br>(69.00) | 148<br>(49.33) |
| No | 30<br>(48.39) | 57<br>(41.30) | 24<br>(24.00) | 111<br>(37.00) |
| No response | 24<br>(38.71) | 10<br>(7.25) | 7<br>(7.00) | 41<br>(13.67) |
| Total | 62<br>(100.00) | 138<br>(100.00) | 100<br>(100.00) | 300<br>(100.00) |

however, admitted that despite their being against dowry practices, they were not able to change the social customs. On the other hand, a few respondents from the lower class admitted that dowry was increasing in their families rather than decreasing.

The respondents of the upper class (48.39 per cent) and of the middle class (41.30 per cent) opine that Doordarshan programmes against dowry would have no impact, unless the status of women changes. The respondents of the lower class (24 per cent) felt that with the increasing materialism, dowry was also increasing. Hence, television content should deplore materialism, only then some change would take place with regard to the practice of dowry. A few respondents, on the other hand, were of the opinion that the practice of dowry was rooted in our social customs and unless they were changed dowry would persist. They further opined that until marriage remained under the domain of elders the practice of dowry would continue, despite propaganda against dowry shown on television.

**Drug Abuse**

The abuse of drug has become worldwide phenomenon. Different explanations have been advanced for the increase in the incidence of drug addiction and there is no consensus among the social scientists regarding the factors which lead to drug addiction. There is, however, a consensus among them with regard to the consequences of drug addiction. The abuse of drug adversely affects the human body and jeopardises individual's capacity to work. Further, it is associated with smuggling and other criminal activities. The Government of India has taken special precautions to check

**TABLE 4.5: Perception of the respondents class-wise that Doordarshan contents were making people aware about the problem of drug abuse**

| | Classes | | | |
|---|---|---|---|---|
| Drug abuse | Upper | Middle | Lower | Total |
| Yes | 14<br>(22.59) | 60<br>(43.48) | 67<br>(67.00) | 141<br>(47.00) |
| No | 23<br>(37.09) | 50<br>(36.23) | 25<br>(25.00) | 98<br>(32.67) |
| No response | 25<br>(40.32) | [illegible]<br>(20.29) | 8<br>(08.00) | 61<br>(20.33) |
| Total | 62<br>(100.00) | 138<br>(100.00) | 100<br>(100.00) | 300<br>(100.00) |

the menace of drug peddaling and addiction. Television as a medium has been used to acquaint the population of its adverse consequences so that people refrain from falling into the habit of using drug.

Sixty-seven per cent respondents of the lower class, 43.48 per cent of the middle class and 22.59 per cent of the upper class admitted that they became more aware about the drug abuse after watching Doordarshan programmes. The respondents of the lower class contended that television programmes had helped them not only to know the bad consequences of the drug abuse, but also its associated problems and consequences. They became more aware about the sources of availability of drugs and how unscrupulous people tried to entice the younger generation into this habit. They had become very cautious and kept a keen watch on their children, so that their children did not come under the influence of drug peddlars. The respondents of the middle and upper classes admitted that it was through television serials that they came to know how drugs were distributed in schools and colleges and children became victims of drugs. They have started keeping an eye on the routines of their children, their friendship circle, as well as their dietary habits.

There were, however, approximately one-third of our respondents who pointed out that programmes on television against drug abuse have failed to create awareness among the general public because such programmes simply depicted the consequences of drug abuse and failed to highlight the motivating forces which initiated people to the use of drug. The respondents of the lower segment opined that people took drugs because of ignorance or to kill drudgery of work. Whereas the respondents of the middle and upper classes felt that people used drugs to get rid of boredom and loneliness. They further opined that Doordarshan programmes should be directed on these issues and only then they could serve any purpose.

**Ethnic and Communal Problems**

India is a plural society. People of different faiths enjoy equal rights along with the majority community. Despite linguistic, regional and religious diversities, people in India have been residing together for centuries, and there is a tolerance about the way of life of each other. However, this unity in diversity is sometimes shattered because of different vested interests. The divide on the lines of religions has been witnessed recently in different parts of India. The recent controversy on *Mandir-Masjid* (temple-mosque) issue at

Ayodhya has resulted into a large scale communal violence. Similarly the activities of some misguided youths in Punjab have tried to put a wrench on the traditional kinship relation between Hindus and Sikhs. The Government is very much aware about its responsibility to create congenial circumstances for different ethnic groups to live in peace and harmony. To attain this objective, Doordarshan is being used to propagate communal harmony and also to make people

TABLE 4.6: **Perception of the respondents class-wise that Doordarshan contents were making people aware about the ethnic and communal problems**

| | Classes | | | |
|---|---|---|---|---|
| Ethnic problems | Upper | Middle | Lower | Total |
| Yes | 20<br>(32.26) | 69<br>(50.00) | 73<br>(73.00) | 162<br>(54.00) |
| No | 30<br>(48.39) | 40<br>(28.99) | 10<br>(10.00) | 80<br>(26.67) |
| No response | 12<br>(19.35) | 29<br>(21.01) | 17<br>(17.00) | 58<br>(19.33) |
| Total | 62<br>(100.00) | 138<br>(100.00) | 100<br>(100.00) | 300<br>(100.00) |

aware about the vested interest of certain political parties to create a division among them. The respondents were asked, whether they were influenced by such programmes shown on television.

Seventy-three per cent respondents of the lower class, 50 per cent of the middle class and 32.26 per cent of the upper class contended that television programmes have helped them to understand in a better way the problems associated with ethnicity and communal violence i.e. how politicians for political gains played with the lives of individuals and used ethnic and communal divide for creating division in the society. In which way communal frenzy resulted into violence disturbing the peaceful co-existence between different communities. The television serials and programmes have helped the respondents to understand the root cause of ethnic and communal problems being faced by our society. They admitted that Doordarshan had played an important role not only in making the people more aware about different problems associated with pluralistic society like India and the mechanism to be adopted to counter hatred among people of different faiths. Most of the respondents of the lower class admitted that during such strifes it was the lower segment who suffered the most. Hence, they should take precautions for peaceful co-existence. The members of the middle and lower classes who became more aware about ethnic problems, contended that different television serials have helped them not only to know about the way of life of other ethnicities but have also helped in developing greater tolerance in them.

A good proportion of the respondents of the upper class (48.39 per cent) and approximately 29 per cent of the middle class and 10 per cent from the lower class contended that television contents failed to create communal harmony because there was a tendency on the political party in authority to use television for defaming the opposition parties for communal violence. They further opined that unless television has autonomy they would not get the objective picture of different happenings. The members of the upper class were highly critical of the television media with regard to its coverage and twisted information, which was given on television pertaining to happenings in Punjab, Jammu and Kashmir and other parts of India. They felt that television instead of informing them misinformed them about the basic facts. It was one of the reasons for them to get links for cable networks so that they could get an objective picture.

**Status of Women**

For centuries women have suffered different discriminations and exploitations. They remained dependent on men. As a child they remained dependent on their father, after marriage on their husbands and in their old age on their sons. They did not enjoy any independent status. Women in rural areas worked in the family labour and under the supervision of menfolk. It is only recently that after attaining education and being equipped with other skills they are engaged in different occupations in urban centres and have independent source of income. After independence different social legislations were passed to grant them equal rights, as enshrined in our Constitution. Despite legal provisions, educational facilities and job opportunities,women still suffer from different types of discriminations. Latest technological development for determining deficient pregnancy is being misused for determining the sex of the unborn. It is reported that people go for abortions if sex of unborn child is female. Different women voluntary organisations and other welfare agencies have recently taken up the cause of women and are creating awareness among the Indian people to check fecticide of the female child. Television in India has also taken up the cause of the female child and with the help of different clippings, documentaries and serials, is trying to educate the Indian population regarding the importance of female child as well as for the removal of different discriminatory practices against women. To what extent Doordarshan programmes have been successful to convey the desired message to the television viewers?

Discrimination based on sex has attracted the attention of a majority of our respondents, particularly of the middle and upper classes. The television clips depicting discrimination against girl child with regard to education, health, food etc. have made the viewers of the middle and upper classes shudder. They became more aware about the discriminatory practices being indulged in against the female child, particularly in the rural areas. Nevertheless, they have become more cautious after seeing television serials and that they would remove discriminatory practices in their families against the female child if there was any. The respondents of the lower class were influenced by the television clips in which it was shown that, the lactating mother was not given nutritious and balanced diet simply because she had given birth to a female child. They admitted that in their families the female child was expected to extend helping hand in family chores as well as to look after the younger siblings, whereas the male child was free to engage in play activities. Despite their willingness to give equal education to the female child they could not do so because of their limited resources. They confessed that they themselves were engaged in discrimination against female child. However, after watching the television clips and serials they have started looking after the female child properly. Further, television serials and discussions have helped them to understand in better manner about property and other rights which have been given to women. Secondly, they were better equipped with legal rights to fight against any discrimination, particularly at the work site. They contented that through television programmes they came to know about equal pay for equal work. They themselves were suffering from this type of discrimination and they were now exerting to get equal wages. Similarly, they have come to know about their rights in their parental property.

There were approximately 30 per cent of the respondents who contended that television had failed to make people aware about the problems of Indian women. They contended that even the educated Indian women preferred to have a male child, because of their belief that it was through the male child that family tree would continue and the male child would provide them security during the old age. They felt that unless bias in favour of male child was removed, Indian women would continue to suffer. Television programmes have failed to touch on this vital issue, hence had no impact on removing the discriminations against the girl children. They further contended that television serials and movies shown on television depicted women in their traditional role, hence instead of bringing about change,television was reinforcing the submissive position of women.

**Social Evils of Indian Society**

The Indian society is marked by ignorance, illiteray and poverty. Further, division of society on caste line has created different cleavages which instead of creating tolerance, has resulted into hatred and exploitation. Doordarshan has taken up an important role to highlight these problems through different serials so that people become aware about the problems of Indian society and take necessary steps to overcome these shortcomings

Among the respondents of the lower class 68 per cent contended that they became more aware about the problem of exploitation of the lower caste people by the landlords in rural India through different serials of television. They came to know how rural poor and illiterate were exploited by the Zamindars (Landlords) by snatching away their small land holding on one pretext or another. They became more aware about the non-availability of formal institutions in rural India for seeking loans to meet different social needs and how the rural people became victim of the landlords of the village. They however lamented their helplessness in eradicating these evils. However, they have formed negative attitudes against the village landlords and were very much against inequality based on caste system. Approximately 50 per cent of the respondents of the middle class contended that they came to know about the problems of rural India through Television serials. Similarly, 46.78 per cent respondents of the upper class admitted that they were completely ignorant about the type of exploitation which existed in rural India and the absolute povertyunder which people were residing. They admitted that television serials were very helpful in making them aware about the extent of illiteracy and ignorance of the rural people and they felt depressed after seeing the serials dipicting the life of the rural poor. A few respondents of the upper and middle classes informed that after watching such programmes on Doordarshan they became members of the voluntary organisations and went to the adjoining villages of Chandigarh so that they could render some service to the needy persons.

The respondents who perceived that television had failed to bring about the desired results with regard to the removal of different evils of the Indian society, felt that social customs could not be changed overnight and particularly when no concrete steps were suggested for bringing about change in the age old traditions. They futher opined that people watched these serials for entertainment and killing time and not for implementing or practising. They further opined that even four decades after independence, primary education was not made compulsory. Caste still played an important role for kinship alliances and political gains. They opined that serials which failed to depict the reality would leave no imprint on people. They further asserted that people would not change their traditions by simply watching advertisements and clippings on Doordarshan. According to them television was not a magic rod which could change the Indian society and its cultural ethos overnight. The change has to be slow and it is possible only when the root cause is highlighted and practical measures are suggested for removing these evils from Indian society. According to them television programmes have failed to touch the basic issues, hence have no impact on the life style of the people.

**Political Awareness**

Television through its coverage of different events informs the general public about the happenings in our country. Indirectly, it also makes the television viewers conscious about the political developments taking place. The news coverage of different incidences, agitations, strikes, communal violence and programmes like, focus, current affairs etc., implicitly create greater political awareness among the public. No doubt, the political party in power uses Doordarshan to project its own image. Nevertheless, the news coverage and coverage of other happenings indirectly create political awareness. We were interested to find out whether television in India has also played a political role i.e., to create political awareness among the television viewers.

TABLE 4.7: Perception of the respondents class-wise that Doordarshan contents were bringing political awareness

| Political awareness | Classes | | | Total |
|---|---|---|---|---|
| | Upper | Middle | Lower | |
| Yes | 35 (56.45) | 92 (66.67) | 41 (41.00) | 168 (56.00) |
| No | 20 (32.26) | 30 (21.74) | 30 (30.00) | 80 (26.67) |
| No response | 7 (11.29) | 16 (11.59) | 29 (29.00) | 52 (17.33) |
| Total | 62 (100.00) | 138 (100.00) | 100 (100.00) | 300 (100.00) |

A majority of the respondents of the upper class (56.45 per cent) and the middle class (66.67 per cent) felt that they became more aware about intricacies of politics after watching different television coverage. The members of the upper and middle classes contended that after watching self-immolation by the young students on 'News Track' they became more aware about the implications of the recommendations of 'Mandal Commission'. They became more knowledgeable about the design of Mr. V.P. Singh (Ex-Prime Minister of India) for dividing the Indian society on the basis of caste for creating a vote bank for his party. They felt that the impact of 'News Track' depicting self-immolation was immense not only because of its access to the public but because of its immediacy and visual drama, the event in question left on the minds of the people. They became very angry with the Government and started hating the leaders who were responsible for forcing the young children to commit suicide. Similarly, they opined that 'Rath Yatra' (Journey by Chariot) of Mr. Advani (Leader of Bharatiya Janata Party) gave them the impression that he was creating a public opinion for the construction of Rama Temple at Ayodhya. However, after watching 'News Track' showing Police atrocities on 'Kar sevaks' (Volunteers for the construc tion of temple) and the role played by the leaders of Bharatiya Janata Party and Vishwa Hindu Parishad, they came to know that the whole episode was motivated for political purposes i.e., to divide the Indian population on the basis of religion to negate the attempts of V.P. Singh Government to divide the electorate on the basis of castes. They were surprised to find out the extent to which our political leaders could go for retaining their position even at the cost of peace and welfare of the country.

The serials on Punjab and Kashmir made them more aware about the role of a foreign country in creating the problem of the terrorism in our country and how the misguided and frustrated youths have fallen prey to the ill designs of the foreign country. The respondents of the lower class (41 per cent), on the other hand, felt that political leaders in India were not sincere and they were never interested in the upliftment of the lower segments of society. The opined that the political leaders did not hesitate to use the idol of 'Rama' for the purpose of seeking votes. They admitted that television has created a new galaxy of heroes and heroines. The success of 'Ramayana' on the small screen prompted the Congress party to use the hero of Ramayana (Arun Govil in the role of Rama) for influencing the voters in its favour and Bharatiya Janata Party has also used Sita and Ravan for getting Lok Sabha seats. The members of the upper and middle classes also identified the serials of Ramayana and Mahabharatha and held that these two serials were responsible for revivalization of Hinduism and political parties like BJP has fully exploited the religious sentiments of the people for their vested interest. They felt that focus, discussion, talks and news coverages on television and video cassettes have made them more aware about manipulative politics and the role our political leaders were playing and they felt disgusted with the political leaders.

A little more than one-fourth of our respondents, however, felt that television has failed to create political awareness among the television viewers, because of its biased and twisted coverage of different events. They opined that television being under the control of the government has failed to inform the people truthfully and objectively. They, however, praised the efforts being made by independent agencies to give greater coverage to the happenings which depicted them objectively. It was for this reason that they were relying more on 'News Track' and other cassettes and Newspapers to find out the reality. A few respondents informed that they relied more on British Broadcasting Corporation (BBC), CNN and other cable transmission rather than the news coverage on Doordarshan.

**National Integration**

Indian society is marked by different diversities. There are number of regional languages, different styles of life, food habits and customs. All these diversities create different divisions in the Indian society. Despite these diversities the cultural ethos and values provide a unifying force and people have learnt to remain united for a national cause. This was very much evident when people of different faiths united for attaining independence. Television as a medium for bringing about new things and changing the style of life also acts as a unifying force through its programmes depicting the great Indian heritage, sports events in which the national team is involved as well as through other serials and coverages. Television is expected to create greater tolerance about others' way of life and national integration.

A majority of the respondents of the upper and middle classes (66.13 per cent and 65.22 per cent respectively) and 39 per cent of the lower class admitted that television in India has an integrative influence in the society. They felt that the screening of international sports in which Indian team also played designated a common and uniform experience. Such television events cross the boundaries that make groups distinct. However, intensely personal the viewing of such events may be, they also constitute the symbols by which people express a common interest and on which social cohesion rests. The respondents indicated that the live telecast of the celebration of 'Republic day' (26th January) parade every year not only made each viewer aware about the progress our country has made, but has also made them proud of the country and has resulted into the development of sense of belongingness. This was more true at the national events whenever sports men and women won international events and National flag of India was shown.

The respondents of the upper and middle class further identified the television clippings, depicting songs, dresses of different regions of India sponsored by Public Relations Department as responsible for creating National Integration and they felt proud that our country was so rich in national resources, songs, drama, music and felt the rhythm of unity in diversity. A few members of the middle class indicated that patriotic songs shown on television have also helped in promoting national integration. The respondents of the upper and middle classes felt that television serials in Hindi shown at the prime time (9.00 p.m.), when all the regional television centres are hooked up to National Programme, have created tolerance for national language even in the regions where people do not understand Devnagri script. They opine that it is through such interesting programmes that national language can be developed and will promote greater integration.

There was, however, a minority group (24 per cent) which felt that television has failed to generate national integration. No doubt, regional films are shown on the national programmes, people do not watch these programmes because they could not understand the language. They further opine that unless we have one national language, we will not be able to promote a national feeling. They contended that the recent happenings in Punjab, Jammu & Kashmir and Assam etc. were leading towards division of

Indian society, rather than creating integration. They further opined that television had failed to generate national integration because of the divide and rule policy of the political party in authority and the way in which television in India had been used. Indirectly, they resented the State control over television coverage and its lack of objectivity and truthfulness.

In the first section of the chapter television viewers were asked to identify important social issues which were taken up in the programme contents of Doordarshan. They were also asked to give their views regarding the effectiveness of such programmes. The television viewers identified a number of social problems like, population, health, age at marriage, dowry, drug abuse, ethnic and communal problems, status of Indian women and other social evils of Indian society like, poverty, illiteracy, ignorance, caste system and the problem of national integration.

A majority of the viewers felt that Doordarshan through its varied programmes had helped them to become more aware about different social problems being faced by our society. Such programmes have brought about changes in their attitudes and behaviour. Additionally, Doordarshan played a significant role in the dissemination of Information regarding their political design and they became politically more aware. However, the impact was differentially perceived by the viewers belonging to different social classes. The viewers who did not perceive the desired effects of such programmes made a number of suggestions for the improvement in the programme contents. In short, Doordarshan has been very successful with regard to its function of information dissemination and the viewers were quite appreciative of its efforts in the right direction.

## Section B

### Evaluation of the Functioning of Television in India

As already stated television in India is controlled by the

State.The programme contents, news items, serials etc. are censored by the government before they are transmitted to the public. The political party in authority has complete control over the medium and would like to depict its own version instead of allowing free flow of information to the public. Further, State control would adversely affect the people's right to be informed freely and objectively and there are chances that only twisted and biased information is given. Several attempts have been made during the last two decades to rectify the flaws in the exising set-up for Radio and Television in India. Different committees were constituted to suggest ways and means by which these two mass media become autonomous. The Chanda Committee in 1969 recommended an independent public corporation for Aakashvani and Doordarshan. The Government, however, took the stand that the time was not ripe for transferring the All India Radio into an autonomous Corporation. The Verghese Committee which was appointed in 1977 submitted its report in 1978 and recommended an autonomous trust to be called 'Aakash Bharati' be set up to control the activities of both Radio and Television. The 'Prasar Bharati Bill' was introduced in 1979 and the bill which was to come up for discussion could not be taken up because parliament was dissolved before the fixed date, and the bill lapsed. In 1982, a working group on software for Doordarshan was set up headed by Dr. P.C. Joshi. In its report submitted in 1985 the group criticised Indian television for disseminating consumarist values rather than promoting general developmental values and orientation. The group wanted the hierarchical bureaucratized and standardized procedural routine of the media production system replaced by an organisation, so that creativity and innovation might be encouraged. The Union Government proposed to set up a single autonomous corporation known as Prasar Bharati (Broadcasting Corporation of India) with two distinct wings, Television and Radio to ensure its working in a fair, objective and creative manner. The bill was introduced on December 29, 1989 to confer autonomy on Television and Radio. The Prasar Bharati Bill introduced in 1989 is a pale shadow of the bill introduced in 1979. Evidently, the political parties in power have had second thought on relaxing official control over the media. The detailed objective set down for the Corporation include the upholding of both the unity and integrity of the country as well as democratic and social values enshrined in the Constituation. The Prasar Bharati Bill safeguards the citizens rights to be informed freely, truthfully and objectively, helping the upliftment of women, combating exploitation, inequality and untouchability, advancing the welfare of weaker sections, safeguarding the rights of working classes and advancing their welfare and protecting the interest of children, handicapped and other vulnerable sections. No doubt, the tasks set before the Corporation are laudable yet the way in which the control of the government is still retained, defeats the very purpose for granting autonomy to Television and Radio (Competition Master, Sept., 1990).

The last part of the chapter deals with viewers, evaluation of the functioning of Doordarshan. The viewers after watching different programmes must have formed certain opinion about the objectivity of Doordarshan contents as they are fullly aware that television in India is State controlled. We are interested to know whether they are interested to give autonomy to Doordarshan or they have certain apprehension that this medium will be misused by multinationals and big business houses. It was for this reason that respondents were asked, whether tiey were in favour of having private channels? If yes, what benefits they would derive from private channels and autonomous Television Corporation?

TABLE 4.8: Distribution of the respondents favouring autonomy to Doordarshan

| Autonomy to Doordarshan | Classes | | | Total |
|---|---|---|---|---|
| | Upper | Middle | Lower | |
| Yes | 42<br>(67.74) | 70<br>(51.22) | 31<br>(31.00) | 143<br>(47.67) |
| No | 20<br>(32.26) | 68<br>(48.78) | 69<br>(69.00) | 157<br>(52.33) |
| Total | 62<br>(100.00) | 138<br>(100.00) | 100<br>(100.00) | 300<br>(100.00) |

More than two-thirds of the respondents of the upper class and a little more than 51 per cent of the middle class and only 31 per cent of the respondents of the lower class were in favour of granting autonomy to Doordarshan and were in favour of having private channels. Those who were in favour of autonomy felt that the quality of programmes shown on Doordarshan would improve. The respondents of the upper and middle classes felt that the information given on Doordarshan would be objective and was not likely to be twisted. They were very much critical of Indian television and its contents. During the Congress rule television in India became "Rajiv Darshan" and when National Front came into power it became "V.P. Singh Darshan", subsequently it turned out to be "Shekhar Darshan", and at present it is beaming "Congress--Panja", they lamented. The respondents were also critical about Doordarshan coverage. They opined that one could see only governmental version of the events or what the ministers said. They relied more on newspapers and magazines rather than Doordarshan for objective information. Some of the respondents having links to cable networks informed us that for getting objective and wider coverage they were relying more on cable transmission. Moreover cable networks provided different channels and they could select any one according to their interests. It was due to non-availability of multiple channels of

Doordarshan that they had opted for cable networks. Further, with the availability of the private channels there would be constructive competition and the viewers could choose out of the multiple programmes being shown at a given period of time. These respondents of the upper and middle classes were highly critical about the quality of Doordarshan programmes which they felt had decreased over the years instead of showing improvement and beaming interesting, entertaining and informative programmes. The respondents of the lower classs felt that with the availability of multiple channels they would have a greater variety of entertaining programmes rather than being exposed to only 'enforced viewing'.

The respondents who were not in favour of granting autonomy to television and having private channels felt that there would be greater control over television of the big businesss houses and television would be used for the promotion of materialistic values in the society. The respondents of the upper and middle classes were apprehensive that such a television would promote obscenity and vulgarity and would promote Western Culture. The members of the middle class were particularly apprehensive that television transmission would come under the control of big business houses who would make use of this powerful medium for the promotion of materialistic values in our society. The members of the lower class, on the other hand, felt that they would be forced to pay for viewing programmes of private channels whereas under the present system they were not required to pay any fee for television viewing. They also felt that commercials would overshadow all other programmes and television contents would become less interesting. However, if their apprehensions, that they would be forced to pay for television viewing, are removed they would prefer private channels and would favour granting autonomy to Doordarshan in India.

Based on the evaluation by the respondents regarding

the information given on Indian television it can be safely concluded that television in India has failed to give unbiased and objective information and respondents, particularly of the upper and middle classes were in favour of granting autonomy to Doordarshan.

The viewers who had links with cable networks were further asked to evaluate programme contents of Doordarshan vis-a-vis cable transmission. Their reactions were almost equally divided. The respondents, who favoured cable transmission over Doordarshan, contended that cable transmission provided them greater coverage, variety of programmes and its news were more objective. Others while endorsing these qualities of cable networks, were of the opinion that cable network transmission was promoting western materialism and obscenity and was eroding Indian cultural ethos.

Taking into account the professed functions of television in India, which is State controlled, it can be concluded that television through its different programmes has been disseminating information to acquaint the people about varied problems being faced by our society. Television has become a powerful medium in moulding public opinion and the viewers wanted from Doordarshan to beam more interesting, informative and entertaining programmes. However, people with different backgrounds perceived the information dissemination function of television differently. Their interpretations of the same programme contents were coloured by their class background. Similarly their evaluation of television content differed. The members of the upper and middle classes, who were more informed, were in favour of granting autonomy to television implying thereby that they were not satisfied with its information coverage, objectivity and performance. The members of the lower class were also in favour of granting autonomy to Doordarshan provided they were not asked to pay for television viewing. In short, it can be concluded that television in India has, no doubt, become a powerful tool for information dissemination and creating public awareness yet information disseminated lacked objectivity and variety. Doordarshan does not face immediate threat from cable networks because its programmes are oriented to the need of our society. However, it has to improve the quality of its programmes and has to make provision for multi-channels beaming different entertaining and informative programmes.

# 5

# A Resume

The main thrust of the study was to find out the effects of television watching on the viewers having different social class background. The impact of television watching was seen with regard to intra and inter-family social interaction as well as on the children who were likely to be the most vulnerable section among the viewers. Attempts were also made to find out the extent to which exposure to Doordarshan programme had created awareness among the viewers regarding different social issues as well as the nature of changes that might have taken place in their attitudes and behaviour patterns with regard to the social issues. The viewers opinions were sought with regard to granting of autonomy to Doordarshan. The programme contents of Doordarshan were also got evaluated. Additionally, the television watchers who had access to cable network were asked to indicate their motivations for seeking cable networks and the expected effects of being exposed to foreign transmission.

As a preliminary step the sample was divided according to living arrangements. One or two room apartments were treated as lower type; residential accommodation with three and four rooms was designated as middle category and houses with five and more rooms were called as upper type. A sample of 100 cases from type of houses was selected subject to the condition that the household had at least one television set and children were also residing with their parents.

For the purpose of re-distribution of the sample according to social class background association between income, occupation and education of the male head of the household was worked out. The value of gamma indicated a high level of association among these variables, that is, persons who had high educational qualifications, were engaged in occupations of high prestige and were also earning high income. However, for the purpose of determining their social class background a composite index was worked out. For this purpose each achieved variable was divided into three divisions and appropriate scores were assigned. For example, income up to Rupees 2000 per month was treated as low and score of one was assigned; income ranging between 2001 to 5000 was given score two and income more than Rupees 5000 was treated as high income and was assigned the score of three. In this manner on all the three variables the score of a person could range between 3 to 9. Those who scored 3 and 4 were treated as belonging to lower class. On the other hand, score of 8 and 9 indicated upper class. The score of the middle class ranged between 5 and 7. In this way the sample was redistributed. Accordingly, there were 100 households from lower class, 138 from middle and 62 from upper class. The class background of the viewers was treated as independent variable to explicate the impact of television viewing.

With regard to family television style it was noted that placement of television sets and sitting arrangements for watching television programmes varied according to the class background of the respondents. Children in the families of lower class normally sat on the floor whereas elders occupied chairs or sat on the cots. In case of the viewers of the middle and upper classes such differentiation was not noted.

Taking into account the duration of time span since the respondents were in possession of televsion sets, it was found that a majority of the viewers of the upper and middle classes had been possessing television sets for the last 10 years or more. On the other hand, a majority of the respondents of the lower class bought their sets recently, that is, during the last 9 years or less. Similarly, a majority of the middle and upper classes respondents had coloured television sets whereas a majority of the respondents of the lower class possessed black and white television sets. As compared with one-third of the households of the upper class possessing two or more television sets, only 18 per cent of the households of the middle class had two sets and not a single respondent of the lower class owned two television sets. The class differences also became evident with regard to the possession of VCR/VCP. As compared with 64 per cent of the upper class only 10 per cent households of the lower class had VCR/VCP. Similar pattern was noticed with regard to accessibility of cable networks. Out of 64 households in the sample who had connections for cable transmission, 22 were from the upper class, 37 from middle class and only 5 were of lower class.

Duration of time spent on watching Doordarshan programmes was also found to be related with the class background of the respondents. The members of the lower class watched television for a longer duration as compared with the family members of the middle and upper classes because television transmission provided them cheapest mode of entertainment. Women from all the classes spent more time on television viewing as compared with men. The sex differences are attributed to the fact that a majority of the women respondents were not engaged in paid work outside their houses. Additionally, even those women who were engaged in paid work on an average spent more time inside the house as compared with men. The afternoon transmission was more common among the women of the middle class families in contrast to the upper class and lower classes.

With the exception of a few families of the upper and middle classes who had VCR/VCP and two or more television sets or accessibility to cable transmission, television viewing was found to be family activity. It became more evident when movies, *chitrahaar* and serials were shown on Doordarhsan. Similarly, Doordarshan programmes shown on Sunday attracted all the members of the household. Television viewing pattern in the upper and middle classes who had two or more television sets and accessibility to cable transmission, was relatively individual based. The availability of different channels on cable networks provided an opportunity to the members to watch programmes of their liking and according to free time at their disposal.

The viewers from the upper and middle classes families who owned VCR/VCP or had links with cable transmission either switched off the television sets when Doordarshan programmes were not according to their liking or used their VCR/VCP or transmission from cable networks to watch programmes of their interest. They further opined that with the exception of a few, most of the programmes shown on Doordarshan were not interesting. Cable transmission not only gave them a choice of multi-channels but also provided them a variety of entertaining programmes. As getting linked to cable networks involves initial investment and monthly charges,members of the lower class have not gone for cable networks. The members of the lower class watched whatever programmes were shown on Doordarshan because of the lack of alternatives, hence for them it was an 'enforced viewing'.

With the exception of watching Doordarshan serials Ramayana' and `Mahabharatha', there was marked difference in the selection of programmes by the families of different classes. Taking into account the professed functions of Doordarshan it was noted that entertaining programmes were liked most followed by informative programmes. Educational programmes of Doordarshan attracted the least number of viewers. Under the entertaining Doordarshan programmes, movies and programmes based on film songs attracted more members of the lower and middle class. On the other hand western music and dances attracted the attention of the young members of the upper class more as compared with other classes. So far as the informative programmes of Doordarshan were concerned, with exception of news, class difference in their selection became evident. Quiz, focus and current affairs on television were watched more by members of the upper and middle classes.

The motivations for viewing different television programmes were also found to be class oriented. The viewers of the lower class watched Doordarshan programmes for entertainment, whereas members of the middle and upper classes treated it as of source of information, education and entertainment.

So far as the effects of television viewing are concerned it was found that a majority of the viewers, irrespective of their class background, had altered their routines, though families of the lower class were affected more. Introduction of television sets has brought about changes in their household work, sleeping and marketing routine. The food was cooked in a hurry and eaten in a given span of time. Late night movies disturbed their sleeping pattern.

The commercials on Doordarshan were watched more by the members of the lower class. However, the exposure to television commercials had differential impact on the viewers having differential class and demographic background. Age related and gender roles become quite evident in the power dynamics of the family with regard to buying behaviour pattern of the viewers. The items of eatables attracted the attention of the younger generation and on their insistence the parents bought those items. The commercials to promote the sale of detergents, soaps, utensils, cookers, cosmetics etc. motivated women in the family. However, costly soaps etc, were bought by women of the upper classes and detergents etc. which were relatively cheap were bought by women of the lower class. Costly items like washing machine, fridge and other durable were bought by men. Similarly investment in insurance and other such schemes advertised on television came under the domain of male heads.

Commercials shown on Doordarshan have created a felt need among the viewers. However, buying advertized items had adversely effected family budget of the lower and middle classes. Further, inability on the part of the parents to buy advertized items as demanded by their children had created frustration and tensions.

Television viewing has, no doubt, brought the family members physicaly together and provided the members of the middle class a subject for discussion. However, physical proximity has failed to bring about social togetherness as during the transmission of programmes there was no conversation among the members of the family. On the other hand, conversation of any type during the programmes was discouraged.

The results help us to conclude that family television viewing behaviour, selection of the programmes, motivations and effects were class based. The power relations of the family have not been changed with the introduction of television.

Introduction of television in the family has also adversely affected activities outside the family. A majority of the viewers of the lower and the middle classes admitted that introduction of television in their homes has forced them to change and readjust their outside activities so that they did not interfere in their watching some interesting television programmes, on the other hand, a majority of the respondents of the upper class have not changed their routine and attended to social calls outside their families, as they thought that maintenance of social contacts outside were more important than watching television. Hence the class background of the viewers played an important role in adversely affecting their network of social relations outside the family.

With regard to television viewing behaviour pattern of the children the data of our study indicate an inverse relation between social class and amount of time spent by children on watching Doordarshan programmes, that is, the higher the class background the lower the duration of time spent on television watching. The children of the middle and upper classes on the other hand spent more time on watching cable transmission and programmes of their liking on VCR / VCP. Taking into account the total time spent on television watching no appreciable difference was found among the children of different classes.

Television viewing has brought about changes in the daily routine of the children. They have readjusted their play activities and homework so that they could watch interesting Doordarshan programmes. However, a majority of the children of the upper classes have not changed their routine activities, either because they did not collide with Doordarshan programmes or the children were not interested in them. A majority of the children of the lower class while doing their homework watched Doordarshan programmes. The children of the lower class were addicted to television.

The power dynamics in the intra-familial relationship of the middle and upper classes become obvious with regard to framing of rules for watching television programmes by the children. And it is the father in the family who has the power to implement these rules. When to watch, what type of programmes and for what duration the children could watch television came under the control of the parents and they strictly implemented these rules. The parents of the lower class have also framed certain rules but due to space problem they could not effectively implement them. The lack of control over children's television viewing became more evident in case of their watching late night movies which were meant for adults only. Television is becoming a powerful stimulator and has even eroded the authority of the parents of the lower class, even though limited to a small number of cases.

The motivations for the children to watch different Doordarshan programmes also varied according to their class background. The children of the lower class watched television to pass time and for entertainment. They were rather encouraged to watch television so that they could remain at home and did not indulge in fights with their peers. On the other hand, the children of the upper and middle classes watched television programmes for relaxation as well as for getting information and learning new things. The parents encouraged their children to watch quiz, focus, current affairs, sports etc. programmes of Doordarshan to acquaint themselves with the latest developments. The children of the middle and upper classes who had access to cable transmission also watched programmes beamed on foreign transmission.

The educational programmes of television sponsored by U.G.C. attracted very few children. Out of 26 respondents who contended that their children watched University Grants Commission programmes, 25 were from the upper and middle classes.

Commercials shown on television have influenced the children and they persuaded their parents to buy items, particularly eatable, advertized on television. The children of those families who had access to cable transmission were highly influenced by foreign goods shown repeatedly during the programmes.

The effects of television viewing on the children were also perceived differently by the viewers. With regard to positive effects of television watching the viewers of the lower class perceived that with the introduction of television at home their children spent more time inside the home which helped them not to loiter and indulge in different mischiefs. Further, television being the cheapest medium of entertainment had checked truancy. On the other hand, a majority of the respondents of the upper and middle classes felt that things which their children could not understand after reading books could easily comprehend through television programmes. They perceived that television watching had increased the knowledge of their children and had also made them more aware about the recent events.

The respondents have also perceived negative effects of television watching on their children. Television watching has adversely effected their studies, has made them more demanding type and they have become obstinate. The children mature early than their age, they waste time and lack initiative. The perception of the respondents varied according to their class status, nevertheless, they admitted that their children were under the spell of television which had become a powerful medium to influence their children.

Television is a powerful medium through which information regarding different societal issues is disseminated. The process of information transmission was divided into dissemination, interpretation and evaluation. It was assumed that viewers having different social class background would not only perceive television programmes differently but would also attach different meanings. Further, their evaluation of the functioning of television in India would also differ.

A majority of the viewers perceived that after being exposed to different Doordarshan programmes they not only became health conscious but also took some remedial steps. However, the respondents with different social background perceived and interpreted them differently. A majority of the respondents of the lower class became more aware about the importance of vaccinations in checking certain diseases in their children. They also became aware about the significance of green vegetables and clean drinking water. They have become very particular about timely vaccination of their children. A majority of the television viewers of the middle class have also benefited from Doordarshan health oriented programmes. They have become more cautious about balanced diet. Approximately one-third of the viewers of the upper class have also benefited from 'Stay fit exercises' and 'Yoga' programmes of television. They learned different exercises and even practised them when such programmes were shown on television. The class background also played an important role in colouring the perception of those who did not feel that television contents were very helpful in creating health awareness. The viewers of the lower class treated the programmes as being highly elitist. On the other hand, the respondents of the upper and middle classes opined that programmes of Doordarshan should take up the issue of the removal of poverty and ignorance to create health awareness among the Indian masses.

Increase in the population was another issue which attracted the attention of the viewers. A majority of the television watchers of the lower class, approximtely half of the middle class and one-fourth of the upper class became more aware about population problem of India after having been exposed to Doordarshan programmes. The viewers of the lower class were influenced by the programmes indicating the significance of spacing between two children and had started using family planning measures. A few had even gone for sterilization. They, however, admitted that they could do so only with the permission of their husbands. The respondents of the upper and middle classes who were already aware about the importance of small family norms felt that unless preference for the male child was not removed, people would continue to have more children.

Television programmes relating to age at marriage was another issue which attracted the attention of more than three-fourths of the viewers of the lower class. They were very much influenced by a programme in which adverse effects of early marriage on the health of the mother and child were shown. They wanted to marry their children only at the optimum age but lamented their helplessness because decisions regarding marrying children were taken by their husbands. The respondents of the upper and middle classes were not confronted with the problem yet they suggested that television programmes for raising the age of marriage would become meaningful only when social customs encouraging such behaviour pattern were removed.

Dowry related problems shown through different television programmes attracted the attention of a majority of the respondents of the lower and middle classes. They were highly impressed by Doordarshan serials in which evil effects of dowry had been shown. They would very much like to discontinue with the practice but due to the pressures of social customs they could not. The respondents of the upper class were not faced with the problem, nevertheless, they were of the opinion that the practice of dowry can be eliminated only when the status of women was elevated and they become independent, hence Doordarshan programmes should concentrate on the issue of raising the status of women.

A majority of the viewers of the lower class, approximately half of the middle class and about one-fourth of the upper class were made more aware about drug abuse after having been exposed to Doordarshan programmes. It was through the Doordarshan serials that they came to know, how young children were being enticed into this habit. After having seen these programmes they have become very cautious and were keeping a watch on their children. The respondents, however, suggested that Doordarshan programmes should highlight the motivating forces which prompted people to become drug addicts, so that parents could check and prevent their children from such bad habit.

Approximately three-fourths of the lower, half of the middle and one-third of the upper class viewers felt that Doordarshan serials and other programmes have helped them to understand the root cause of ethnic and communal problems and how politicians for their vested interests were creating division in the society. Those respondents who felt that television programmes had failed to promote communal harmony suggested that news and other events should be shown on television objectively. They felt that Doordarshan being under the control of Government, was being used by the political party in power to defame the opposition. Such a situation has adversely affected the creditability of Doordarshan transmission.

Television programmes indicating discrimination based on sex has attracted the attention of a majority of the viewers and they became more aware about different ways in which the female child was discriminated. The respondents from the lower class contended that it was through Doordarshan serials and other women related programmes that they came to know about women's right in property as well as about equal pay for equal work. The viewers were also critical about Doordarshan serials in which women were depicted in their traditional role only. The programmes should highlight different avenues open to women and their success stories so that stereo-typed notions about women were removed from our society.

Television in India through different serials and other

programmes has attacked caste institution and its evils. Similarly, the problems on ignorance, illiteracy, poverty, exploitation of the landless etc. were the subject matter of different Doordarshan programmes. The viewers admitted that they became more aware about these problems after being exposed to television programmes. The lower class respondents have developed hatred against the landlords in the villages and other exploiters of the weaker sections. A few respondents of the upper and middle classes informed that after being motivated by such programmes they became members of voluntary organisations so that they could help the ignorants.

The viewers felt that Doordarshan programmes were also helpful in creating political awareness. After watching different events on television, or through video cassettes they became aware about manipulative politics of our leaders. They felt that different political parties were creating a vote bank in the name of caste, ethnicity and religion. They became aware about the dirty game of the political leaders and have developed a hatred against them.

A majority of the viewers of the upper and middle classes and a little more than one-third of the lower class felt that Doordarshan through different serials and programmes was helpful in promoting national integration. The respondents wanted that television should give greater coverge to national events and should highlight our achievements as a nation as well as our shortcomings so that people could take remedial steps.

The reactions of the viewers regarding the functioning of television in India and their willingness to grant autonomy to television also varied according to their class background. More than two-thirds of the upper class, a little more than half of the middle class and less than one-third of the lower class respondents were in favour of granting autonomy to television. They were very critical about the biased and disinformation given on Doordarshan. They felt that with availability of private channels there would be greater constructive competition and viewers would get unbiased and objective information. The viewers of the lower class felt that they would have a greater variety of entertaining programmes rather than being exposed to only 'enforced viewing'.

The viewers who were not in favour of granting autonomy to Doordarshan, felt that television would come under the control of big houses which would promote materialistic values in our society. They were also apprehensive that obscene and vulgar programmes would be shown on television which would have ill-effects on the younger generation. The members of the lower class were afraid that they would be forced to pay for viewing programmes if control of televison was given to the private concerns.

The viewers who had access to cable networks, found cable transmission more interesting, providing them a variety of programmes to choose from and giving world wide and objective news coverage. In contrast Doordarshan transmission lacked variety and was poor in quality. These viewers also associated negative effects of foreign transmission on their children which was promoting materialism and obscenity. They felt that as foreign television programme contents were devoid of Indian cultural ethos, cable network would not be able to pose any serious threat to Doordarshan.

With the help of the results of the study we can now answer the research questions with which the present study was started.

1. Family television viewing behaviour pattern varies according to the class background of the viewers. Members of the lower class watched television programmes for longer duration.
2. Entertainment was the main motivating factor for women, children and members of the lower class to watch Doordarshan programmes, whereas the members of the upper and middle classes treated television medium as a source of information and education in addition to its being for entertainment.

3. The viewers perceived both positive and negative effects of television watching on their routine family activities. However, their perception varied according to their class background. The members of the lower class have brought about changes in cooking, eating and sleeping behaviour pattern. No appreciable change was noticed among the viewers of the upper class.

4. Family power relations became evident with regard to handling of television sets, sitting arrangement, buying advertized goods. The families of the lower class exhibited stereo-typed gender and age related role relations, that is, husband / father played a dominant role.

5. With the exception of a few families of the middle and upper class which had two or more television sets, television viewing was a family activity. No doubt, television watching facilitated physical proximity of the family members but did not encourage communication. Introduction of television has facilitated greater interaction between the neighbours of the lower class where in the families of upper class, it has neither encouraged or hindered their social interactions inside and outside their families.

6. The children of the lower class families spend more time on watching Doordarshan programmes. The children of the middle and upper classes who had access to cable transmission and had VCR / VCP spent more time on watching programmes of their liking. No appreciable difference was noticed with regard to total time spent on television watching. The children of the middle and upper classes have adjusted their routine so that their routine activities are not disturbed. The parents have framed rules and regulated their children television viewing and these rules were implemented more strictly among the upper and middle class families. The parents of the lower

class could not regulate their children's viewing behaviour because of lack of space.

7. The children of the lower class were attracted to television programmes for entertainment whereas the children of the middle and upper classes in addition to using it for entertainment also found it useful for information and educative purposes. Children were highly influenced by television commercials which created a felt-need in them, particularly, with regard to eatable goods advertized on television. Failure on the part of the parents to buy the advertized goods as demanded by their children created tension in the families of the lower classes.

8. The parents perceived both positive and negative effects of television viewing on their children, however, their perception of both positive and negative effects varied according to their class background. The members of the lower class opined that their children used to loiter around and indulged into different mischiefs and quarrels. With the television at home their children have started spending more time inside the house and hence have been saved from bad company. The parents of the middle and upper classes felt that their children learnt many new things from television transmission. Things which their children could not understand and remember after reading books could now be easily comprehended. Similarly their perception with regard to negative effects of television watching on their children differed according to their class background.

9. The parents regulated television watching of their children. When to watch, what to watch and for what duration were controlled by the parents of the middle and upper classes. The parents of the lower class could not implement these rules due to shortage of space. The children of the lower class were motivated

to watch television for entertainment whereas children of the middle and upper classes used it for information in addition to entertainment.

10. Doordarshan programmes proved to be very helpful in making the viewers more aware about different issues and problems of our country. However, the respondents with different class background perceived the effects of television contents differently. Their interpretations, meanings and evaluation of the television contents also varied according to their social class background.

11. Television in India is a medium of entertainment for the members of the lower class whereas it fulfils all the three professed functions for the upper and middle class viewers. More respondents of the upper and middle classes were not satisfied with the quality of Doordarshan programmes. They were highly critical of its being biased and lacking objectivity.

12. A majority of the viewers of the upper and middle classes and only one-third of the lower class did not endorse governmental control over television transmission. They wanted to grant autonomy to television and were in favour of having private channels so that information dissemination was truthfully and objectively done. The viewers of the lower class are apprehensive that once Doordarshan becomes autonomous, they would be forced to pay fee every month.

13. For the sake of getting a variety of programmes to choose and to get objective and unbiased news coverage the respondents of the middle and upper classes have sought links for cable transmission. These viewers were highly critical about the quality of Doordarshan programmes. Nevertheless, they were also appreciative about the role of Doordarshan in making people more aware about the social problems of

our country as well as for its orientation to exhibit Indian cultural ethos.

## Conclusion

With the exception of a few families of the middle and upper classes television viewing was found to be a family activity. No doubt, the members watched television programmes together but lacked social togetherness. Television watching has altered the rhythm of intra and inter-family social interactions. It has become an important agent of socialization particularly for the younger generation. The commercials shown on television have created a felt need among the viewers and children were found to be the most vulnerable to these commercials. The parents were forced to buy things for them and their failure to do so created tension in the family. Nevertheless, the parents still exerted control over television viewing behaviour pattern of their children.

The main motivating force for the members of the lower class to watch television programmes was entertainment whereas the viewers of the middle and upper class treated it as a source of information and entertainment. The social class background of the viewers influenced their perceived positive and negative impact of television watching. Similarly, their perception regarding the functioning of Doordarshan pertaining to information dissemination, their interpretation of the programme contents and evaluation varied according to their social class background. In short, the study supports the 'reciprocal influence' hypothesis.

Doordarshan through its varied programmes has not only made the viewers more aware about different societal problems but has also facilitated changes in their attitudes and behaviour pattern. Doordarshan has successfully created a special place for itself among the viewers. Taking into account the reactions of the viewers, who had access to cable network, Doordarshan does not face immediate threat. Nonetheless, as a long term strategy it has to adopt a professional approach for successfully competing with foreign transmission. If it has to survive it has to improve the quality of its programme contents while making provisions for multiple channels beaming a variety of programmes.

The study partially supports both the "effects" and "uses and gratification" perspectives. The television viewers watched programmes as per their likings and during the free time at their disposal. The right to switch on or off the television set remained with the viewers. To get a clear picture regarding the applicability of these perspectives in our society it is suggested that more scientific studies should be undertaken in different regions and population samples in India.

# APPENDIX

Social class background of the viewers was worked out based on the achieved attributes--income, education and occupation--of the male head of the households. As a first step association between these variables was worked out taking into account the value of gamma. Subsequently each head was assigned scores on all the three variables and depending upon the scores they were divided into three classes.

TABLE 1.1: **Association between Income and Education**

| | | | Education | | | | | |
|---|---|---|---|---|---|---|---|---|
| Income | High | % | Medium | % | Low | % | Total | % |
| High | 32 | 60.38 | 48 | 33.33 | 3 | 2.92 | 83 | 27.67 |
| Medium | 21 | 39.62 | 80 | 55.56 | 28 | 27.18 | 129 | 43.00 |
| Low | | | 16 | 11.11 | 72 | 69.90 | 88 | [illegible] |
| Total | 53 | | 144 | | 103 | | 300 | |

Value of gamma = 0.81

TABLE 1.2: **Association between Occupation and Income**

| | | | Income | | | | | |
|---|---|---|---|---|---|---|---|---|
| Occupation Prestige | High | % | Medium | % | Low | % | Total | % |
| Low | 1 | 1.20 | 30 | 23.25 | 69 | 78.41 | 100 | 33.33 |
| Middle | 31 | 37.35 | 83 | 64.35 | 19 | 21.59 | 133 | 44.34 |
| High | 51 | 61.45 | 16 | 12.40 | | | 67 | 22.33 |
| Total | 83 | | | 129 | 88 | | 300 | |

Value of gamma = 0.86

TABLE 1.3: Association between Occupation and Education

| Occupation Prestige | Education High | % | Medium | % | Low | % | Total | % |
|---|---|---|---|---|---|---|---|---|
| High | 31 | 58.49 | 36 | 25.00 | | | 67 | 22.33 |
| Middle | 18 | 33.96 | 88 | 61.11 | 27 | 26.21 | 133 | 44.34 |
| Low | 4 | 7.55 | 20 | 13.89 | 76 | 73.79 | 100 | 33.33 |
| Total | 53 | | 144 | | 103 | | 300 | |

Value of gamma = 0.81

TABLE 1.4 : Distribution of the head of the households by their scores and type of house

| Score | 1-2 rooms | 3-4 rooms | 5+ rooms | Total |
|---|---|---|---|---|
| 3 | 57 | 2 | -- | 59 |
| 4 | 23 | 18 | -- | 41 |
| 5 | 11 | 11 | 3 | 25 |
| 6 | 9 | 44 | 17 | 70 |
| 7 | -- | 15 | 28 | 43 |
| 8 | -- | 6 | 33 | 39 |
| 9 | -- | 4 | 19 | 23 |
| Total | 100 | 100 | 100 | 300 |

TABLE 1.5: Redistribution of the viewers according to their social classes

| Score | Social Class | Frequency |
|---|---|---|
| 3,4 | Lower | 100 |
| 5,6,7, | Middle | 138 |
| 8,9 | Upper | 62 |
| Total | | 300 |

# REFERENCES

Acharya, R.N. (1987). Television in India. New Delhi, Manas Publications.

Aghi, M.B.(1977). Impact of Science Education Programme on SITE. Children of Rajasthan. Ahmedabad. Space Application Centre.

Agrawal, B.C. (1978). Television Comes to Village: An Evaluation of SITE. Bangalore. Indian Space Research Organisation.

Agrawal, B.C. & M.R. Malek (1986). Television in Kheda. New Delhi. Concept Publishers.

Ahuja, R. (1987). Crimes against women. Jaipur, Rawat Publishers.

Albrecht,M.C. (1954). "The relationship of literature and society" American Journal of Sociology, Vol.LIX, March. pp. 425-436

Atkin, C. (1978). "Observation of Parent Child Interaction in Super Market decision making" Journal of Marketing, Vol. 42, pp.41-45.

Austin, B.A. (1985). "Loneliness and Use of Six mass media among college students" Psychological Reports. Vol 56, pp. 323-327.

Bahl, Neena (1988) "Equalizing Status: Television and Tradition in an Indian Village". In James, Lull (Ed.) World Families watch Television. Beverly Hills, Sage Publications.

Bandura, A. (1973). Aggression: A social learning analysis. Englewood Cliffs, NJ: Prentice Hall.

Bandura, A. (1977). Social learning. Englewood Cliffs, NJ: Prentice Hall.

Bandura, A. (1978). "Social learning theory of aggression" Journal of Communication, 28(3) pp. 12-29.

Bearison, David J., M. Jean & R. Danielle (1982). "Developmental changes in how children understand TV" Social Behaviour and Personality. Vol. 10, No. 2.

Bogart, Leo (1962). "American TV: A Brief Survey of Findings" Journal of Social Issues, Vol. 18, No. 2, March.

Bourdieu, P. (1984). Distinction. London. Routledge & Kegan Paul.

Brody, Gene, M. & Zolinda Stoneman (1883). "The Influence of TV Viewing on Family: A contextualist framework." Journal of Family Issues, Vol. 4, No. 2, June.

Brown, Less (1971). TV: The business behind the box. New York: Harcourt Brace Jovanvich.

Cazeneuve, Jean (1964). "Television and Myths". Social Interaction, 2, 2, pp. 157-168, cited in Socialogical Abstract, Vol. 14, No. 1, Jan. 1966.

Chombart, delauwe & Marie Jose (1985). "Child and TV interaction" Centre national recherche scientifique, 75700, Paris (France) cited in Sociological Abstract, Vol. 34, No. 2, June 1986.

Churchill, Gilbert A., Jr. & P. George Moschio (1979). "TV and interpersonal influences in Adoloscent Consumer Learning", The Journal of Consumer Research, Vol. 6, No. 1.

Churchill, Roberts (1981). "Children's & Parents TV viewing and Perceptions of violence" Journalism Quarterly 58, 4, Winter pp. 556-581 cited in Sociological Abstract, Vol. 31, No. 3, Aug. 1983.

Collins, W.A. (1982). "Cognitive Processing in TV viewing". Communication Research, Vol II, No. 4, Oct.

Competition Master. September, 1990.

Comstock, G. (1978). "Impact of TV on American Institution", Journal of Communication, 28, 2, Spring, pp. 12-28 cited in Sociological Abstract, Vol. 28, No.4, Oct. 1990.

Comstock G. S. Chaffee; N. Katzman; M. McCombs & D. Roberts (1978). Television and human behaviour. New York. Columbia University Press.

Comstock G. (1980). Television in America. Beverly Hills. Sage Publications.

Dahlgren, P. (1977) . cited by Tuchman 1981 "Myth & the Consciousness Industry: A new look at the effects of the mass media" In E. Katz & T. Szecsko (eds) Mass Media and Social Change. London. Sage Publications.

Dahlgren, P. (1981). " TV News and the suppression of Reflexivity". In E. Katz & T. Szecsko (eds) Mass Media and Social Change.London. Sage Publications.

Defleur, Melvin L. & Lois B. Defleur (1967). "The relative contri bution of TV as a learning for Children's Occupational knowledge." American Sociological Review, Vol. 32, No. 5, Oct - pp. 777-789.

Dorr, Annie (1986). Television and Children: A special medium for Special Audience. Beverly Hills , Sage Publications.

Fedler, Fred ( 1978). An Introduction to Mass Media. New York: Harcourt, Brace Inc.

Fiske, John (1989). "Moments of Television: Neither the texts nor the audience." In E. Seiter, H. Borchers, Gabride Kreutzner and Eva Maria Warth (eds). Remote Control. London, Rouledge.

Gerbner, G. (1958). "The Social role of the Confession Magazine." Social Problems, Vol.6. Summer.

Golding, P. (1981) "The Missing Dimensions--News Media and the Management of Social Change" In E. Katz & T. Szecsko (eds) Mass Media and Social Change. London. Sage Publications.

Goodman, I.F. (1983). "Television's role in family interaction." Journal of Family Issue, Vol. 4, pp. 405-424.

Gorn, Gerald J. & Marvin, E. Goldberg (1977). "The Impact of TV advertising on Children from low income families." Journal of Consumer Research, Vol. 4, No. 2, pp.86-88 cited in Sociological Abstract, Vol. 28, No. 1, April, 1980.

Greenberg, B.S; B. Dervin; J. Bowes & J. Dominick (1970). Use of Mass Media by the Poor. New York, Praeger.

Groombridge, Brian (1972). TV and the people, London, Penguin Edition.

Gurevitch, Michael (1971). "TV & Sabbath Culture in Isreal" Jewish Journal of Sociology, 13, 1, June, Cited in Sociological Abstract , Vol. 20, No. 1, 1972.

Hall, S. (1980). "Encoding /Decoding" In S. Hall, D. Hobron, Andrew Lowe & Wills (eds) Cultural Media, Language. London Hutchinson.

Halloran, J. ( ed) (1970). The Effects of Television,London. Panther Books.

Halloran, J. R. L. Brown & D.C. Chaney (1970). Television and Delinquency, London. Leicester, U. Press, cited in Sociological Abstract, Vol. 20, No. 3. 1972.

Hartmann P.; B.R. Patil & Anita Dighi ( 1989). The mass media and Village life: An Indian Study, New Delhi, Sage Publications.

Heath, L; C. Kruttschnitt and D. Ward (1986). TV & Violent Criminal behaviour, Beyond the Bobo doll" Victims & Violence, Vol.1, No. 3, Fall.

Hinde, Robert A. (1979) Social Interaction. London, Accdemic Press, Inc.

Hirsch, P. (1971). " Sociological Approaches to the Pop Music Phenomenon" American Behavioural Scientist, Vol. 14, pp. 371-388.

Holman, J. & V.A. Braithwaite (1982). "Parental life style & Children TV Viewing "Australian Journal of Psychology, 34, 3, pp. 375-382, cited in Sociological Abstract.Vol. 33, No. 3, Oct. 1985.

Howe, Michael (1977). Television and Children, London New University Education.

Jesudasan (1977). Cited by Gupta, G. (1986). " Women & Children Programmes" in Aggarwal B.C. & A.K. Sinha (eds) SITE TO INSAT, New Delhi. Concept Publication Company.

Johnson, N. ( 1967). How to talk back to your TV Set. Boston: Little Brown & Company.

Johnstone, J.W.C. (1974) "Social Integration & Mass Media use among adoloscents ; A case study " In J.G. Blumer & E. Katz (eds) The uses of mass communication; current perspectives on gratification research. Beverly Hills, Sage Publications.

Katz E. & T.Szecsko (1981). Mass Media and Social change. London, Sage Publications.

Kazmier, L. J. (1977). Principles of Management. Bombay Tata McGraw Hill.

Landon, James A. (1962). "Attitudes towards Commercial and Educational TV" Journal of Advertising Research, Vol. 2, No. 3, pp. 33-36 cited in Sociological Abstract, Vol. 12, No. 8, 1964.

Larson, D.N. (1968). Violence and Mass Media. New York. Harper & Row.

Leifer, A.D; W.A. Collins; B.M. Gross; P. H. Taylor, L. Andrews & E.R. Blackman (1971). "Developmental Aspects of Variable relevant to observational learning: Child Development". Communication Research Vol. 11, No. 4, Oct, 1984.

Liebert, R.M. & Joyce Sprafkin (1988). The Early Window Effects of TV on Children & Youth. New York, Pergamon Press.

Lull, James (1980). "Family Communication Patterns and the Social Uses of Television." Communication Research, Vol. 7, No. 3, July.

Lull, James (1982). "How families select television programmes: A mass observational study" Journal of Broadcasting, Vol. 26, No. 4.

Lull, James (ed) (1988). World families watch Television. Beverly Hills, Sage Publications.

Malik, B.P.S. (1986)."The Psychological impact of TV on Children below Twelve" A term paper on B. degree in Mass Communication. Panjab University, Chandigarh.

Mamoria, C.B. (1987). Personal Management. Bombay, Himalya Publishing House.

Martin Serrano, Manuel (1982). "The Social influence of Television sources and methods of Study"Revista, Espanola de Investigations Sociologicas, 17, Jan-Mar. pp. 65-82 cited in Sociological Abstract, Vol. 31, No. 3, Aug. 1983.

Mass Media(1981-83) Ministry of Information and Broadcasting. New Delhi, Government of India Publication.

McCormack, T. (1981). "Revolution Communication and the sense of History" In E. Katz & T. Szecsko (eds) Mass Media and Social Change. London, Sage Publications.

Melody, W.H. (1973). Children's Television: The economics of exploitation. New Haven,Yale University Press.

Morley, D. (1989). "Changing Paradigms in audience Studies" . In E. Seiter; H. Borchers; G. Kreutzner and E. Maria Warth (eds). Remote Control. London, Routledge.

Noelle-Neumann, E. (1981). "Mass Media and Social Change in Developing Societies." In E. Katz & T. Szecsko (eds). Mass Media and Social Change, London, Sage Publications.

Pingree, S; R. Hawkins; D. Rouna; J. Burns; W. Gikonyo and C. Nevwirth (1984). "Another lookat Children's Comprehension of Television" . Communication Research, Vol. II, No. 4, Oct.

Postman, N. (1982). The disappearance of Childhood. New York, Delacorte.

Pourtois, Jean Pierre (1978)."Does TV violence affect aggressive behaviour in children ? "Reseaux, Vol. 32 No. 34, pp. 95-102 cited in Sociological Abstract, Vol. 32, No. 5, Dec. 1984.

Press, Andrea (1989). "Class and Gender in Hegemonic Process: Class difference in women's perceptions of TV realism and identifications with TV Characters". Media, Culture and Society, Vol11, No. 2, April, pp. 229-251 cited in Sociological Abstract, Vol. 38;No. 2, June 1990.

Rainwater, L; R.P. Coleman & G. Handel (1959). Working man's Wife. New York, Oceans Publications.

Reid, Leonard, N. & Charles, F. Frazer (1980). "Children's use of Television Commercials to initiate Social Interaction" Journal of Broadcasting, Vol. 24, No. 2, Spring, pp. 149-158 cited in Sociological Abstract, Vol. 29, No. 4 Oct 1981.

Ritchie, Price Roberts (1987). "Television Reading and Reading Achievements". Communications Research, Vol. 14, No. 3, June.

Roberts, D.F; Christine M. Bachen; Melinda C. Hornby; P. Hernandez Romes (1984). " Reading and Television: Predictors of Reading Achievement at different age levels" Communications Research, Vol, 11, No. 1, Jan.

Robinson, J.P. (1972). "TV's Impact on everyday life", in E.A. Rubinstein; G.A. Comstock & J.P. Murray (eds) Television in Day-to-day life: Patterns of Use. Washington D.C., Govt. Printing Office.

Rogge, Jan-Uwe (1989). "The media in everyday life" In E. Seiter; H. Borchers; G. Kreutzer and Eva Maria Warth (eds) Remote Control. London, Routledge.

Rosengren, K.E.(1981). "Mass Media and Social Change: Some current approaches". In E. Katz & T. Szecsko (eds). Mass Media and Social Change. London, Sage Publications.

Rosengren, K.E. & S. Windahl (1972). "Mass Media as a functional alternative." In D. Mcquail (ed.) Sociology of Mass Communication. Middlesex, England, Penguin.

Root, J. (1986). Open the Box. London, Comedia.

Rossiter, John R. & Thomas S. Robertson (1980)" Children disposition towards proprietary drugs and the role of TV drug advertising." The Public opinion Quarterly Vol 44, No. 3, Fall, pp. 316-329 cited in Sociological Abstract, Vol. 29, No. 5, Dec. 1981.

Roy, Danish (1963). "The American family and Mass Communication" Marriage and Family living. Vol. 25, No. 3.

Schramm, W; J. Lyle and E.B. Parker (1961). TV in the lives of our children. Stanford, C.A. Stanford University Press.

Schramm, W. (1964). Mass Media and National Development. California, Stanford University Press.

Seiter, E; Borchers; G. Kreutzner and Eva Maria Warth (eds) (1989). Remote Control. London, Routledge.

Sharma, V. (1989). "Effects of TV commercials on Children." A term paper for B degree in Mass Communication. Panjab University, Chandigarh.

Shukla, S. and Kumar, Kuldip (1977). SITE impact on Children. Ahmedabad, Space Application Centre.

Singer, D.G. (1982)."TV and developing imaginations of Child" in D. Pearl ; L. Bouthile & J. Dazer (eds). Television and Behaviour, Vol.II. Washington D.C; U.G. Govt, Printing Press.

Singer, D.G & J.L. Singer (1977). "Television: A member of Family" National Elementary Principal, Vol.56, March, pp. 50-53.

Singh, Y. (1977). Social Stratification and Changes. New Delhi, Manohar Publication.

Sinha, A.K. (1985). Mass Media and Rural Development. New Delhi, Concept Publishing Company.

Szalai, A. (ed) (1972). The Usc of time. The Hague, Mouton & Company.

Tannis & Macbeth (1981). "How and What do Children learn from TV" Human Communication Research, Vol. 7, No. 2, cited in Sociological Abstract, Vol. 30, No. 5, Dec. 1982.

The Tribune, Chandigarh (City edition) September 14, 1989.

The Tribune, Chandigarth (City edition) February 17, 1991.

The Tribune, Chandigarh (City edition ) April 25, 1992.

Tuchman, G. (1979). "Women's depiction by the mass media". Signs, Vol. 4, No. 3. Spring.

Tulloch, John & Albert, Moran (1986). A Country Practice: Quality Soap. Sydney, Currency Press.

Vardaman & Halterman (1968). Managerial Control through Communication. New York, John Wiley & Sons.

William, F. (1982). The Communication Revolution. Beverly Hills, Sage Publications

Wilson, S.J. (1981). "The Image of Women in Canadian Magazines" In E. Katz, & T. Szecsko (eds.), Mass Media and Social Change, London, Sage Publications.

Wren-Lewis, J. (1983). "The Encoding/Decoding Model: Criticisms and Redevelopments on Decoding." Media, Culture and Society, Vol.5.

Yadava J.S. & U.V. Reddi (1988). "In the midst of diversity: TV in Urban Indian Homes". In James Lull (ed) World Families Watch Television, Beverly Hills, Sage Publications.

# Index

Age of marriage, 92, 94, 125
Aghi, M.B. 13
Agrawal, B.C., 11
Ahuja, R., 94
Albrcht, M.C., 10
Atkin, C., 67
Austin, B.A., 15
Autonomy to TV :
  Viewer, Views of- 127-8

Bandura, A., 66
Bearison, David. J., 28
Behl, Neena., 11
Bell, 9
Bogart, Leo, 18
Bourdieu, P., 23
Braith Waite, V.A. 18
Brody, Gene, 15
Brown, Les, 49

Cable net work:
  Popularity, 128-9
Cezeneuve, Jean, 19
Children:
  Impact
    Daily routine, 121;
    Commericlas, 75-6
    Television viewing, 77-83;
  Motivation for TV viewing, 73-77;
  TV viewing Behaviour Pattern, 68-72
Chombart, Delauwe, 18
Churchill, Gilbert, A., 19
Collins, W.A., 28
Coloured TV:
  Possession, 37-8
Commercial Services, 49
Commercials:
  Influence,
    Family Budget, 57-8
Comstock, A., 10,15,18,20,66,68,85

Dahlgren, P., 12
Defleur, Melvin L., 18
Doordarshan:
  Afternoon Programmes, 41-43
  News, 48
  Programmes, 38
Dorr, Annie, 10,20,39,66-9,84,86
Dowry, 94, 124
Drug Abuse, 96

Educational Programmes, 47-8
Effects of Television Viewing, 10-14
Effect Theory, 21-22
Ethnic and Communal Problems, 97-9

Evening Programmes:
Entertainment, 44

Family:
Impact, 14, 15, 18
TV viewing Behaviour, 120,121
TV viewing style, 117
Fiske, John, 10,13,22
Functioning of Television in
India Evaluation, 108-114

George, Moschio P., 19
Gerbner, G., 72
Goldberg, Marvin, E., 18
Golding P., 12
Goodman, IF., 15
Gorn, Gerald J., 18
Gupta, G., 11
Gurevitch, Michael, 15

Hall, Stuart:
Model, 23
Halloran, J.R., 19,21
Halterman, 2
Hartmann, P., 11,12,21
Health, Awareness, 87-90,124
Health, L., 19
Hinde, Robert A., 3
Hirsch, P., 10
Holman, J., 18
Howe, Michael, 18

Impact of TV:
Children,
Behaviour Pattern, 66-8
Family,
Aspects, 34

Information dissemination and
its interetation, 87
Information Technology, 9-10

Jesudasan, 11
Johnson, N., 11
Johnstone, J.W.C., 15
Jose, Marie, 18
Jowett, 14

Katz, E., 12
Kazmier, L.J., 2
Kumar, Kuldip., 14

Larsen, D. N., 19
Liefer, A.D., 20
Lower class:
Place of TV in home, 36
Lull, James, 15-16,33-34,84

Mcbeth, 18
Mahabharata, 43-4,46-48,119
Commercials, 49
Malek, M.R., 11
McCormack, T., 10
Melody, William, 49
Middle Class:
Place of TV in home, 36
VCP, 49
Viewing style, 118-119
Morley, D., 13,16,21,24
Motivation for Television
viewing, 45-51,119:
Educational Programmes, 47-8
Entertainment, 46-47
Selection of Programmes, 45-6

National Integration, 106-8

National Programmes, 48
Noelle-Neumann, E., 11-15

O'Donnell, 14

P.C. Joshi Committee, 2
Place of TV in House
  Classwise, 36t
Political awareness, 103-06:
  TV, role of, 127
Population Problem, 90-92,125
Postman, N., 19
Pourtois, Jean Pie, 19

Rainwater, L., 12
Ramayana, 46,48,119
Reddi, UV, 17,39
Ritchie, 28
Robert, D., 20
Robinson, J.P., 11,15
Rogge, Jan-Owe, 16
Rosengren, K.E., 14,15
Roy, Danish, 14

Sarabhai, Vikram, 5
Schramm W., 10,12
Seiter, E., 12
Serials, 46:
  Impact, 126
  Watching of- 119
Shukla, S., 14
Singer, D.G., 36, 67
Singer, J.L., 36
Sinha, A.K., 11-14
SITG, 5
Social Evils of Society, 102-03
Societal Problems:
  Viewers awareness, 132
Sparfkin, Joyce, 11
Status of Women, 99-102
Study:
  Objectives, 24-26
  Results, 128-32
Szalai, A, 15

Tannis, 18
Televisioin:
  as a Medium of learning, 65-7
  Contents, 9
  Development, 4-7
  Functions, 7-9
Tuchman, G., 12
Type of Programmes, 75-6

UGC Programmes, 43,75
Upper Class:
  Doordarshan as entertainment, 1,48
  Place of TV in home, 36-7
  Viewing style, 116-117

Vardaman, 2
VCP, 44-45,48-9,73,82,117,118,121
VCR, 44-45,48-9,73,82,117,118,121:
  Possession, 38
  Social class book ground, 115-116
Viewing of Television:
  Impact,
    Children, 77-83
    Daily routine of children, 121
    Family Relations, 59-60
    Interactions out side
      the family, 60-2,
    Intra family Relations, 122-3
    Style, 35-45
      as Family activity, 34,39-40
      Time, 40-41
      Working Male members, 40-41

William, F., 9
Wilson, S.J., 1,12,13
Windahl, S., 15
Women Viewers:
  Afternoon Programmes, 41,43-44
Wren-lewis, J., 24

Yadava, J.S., 17,39